LIFE IN
NEW YORK

FULCRUM

Library of Congress Cataloging-in-Publication Data

Pedersen, Laura.
  Life in New York : how I learned to love squeegee men, token suckers, trash twisters, and subway sharks / Laura Pedersen.
    pages cm
  ISBN 978-1-936218-15-8 (paperback)
1. Pedersen, Laura. 2. Pedersen, Laura--Homes and haunts--New York (State)--New York. 3. Novelists, American--20th century--Biography. 4. Novelists, American--21st century--Biography. 5. Floor traders (Finance)--United States--Biography. I. Title.
  PS3566.E2564Z46 2015
  818'.5403--dc23
  [B]
                              2015009131

Printed in the United States of America
0 9 8 7 6 5 4 3 2 1

Cover illustration by Alex Asfour
Cover design by Jessica Townsend

Fulcrum Publishing
4690 Table Mountain Dr., Ste. 100
Golden, CO 80403
800-992-2908 • 303-277-1623
www.fulcrumbooks.com

ALSO BY LAURA PEDERSEN

Nonfiction

Play Money

Buffalo Gal

Buffalo Unbound

Planes, Trains, and Auto-Rickshaws

Fiction

Going Away Party

Beginner's Luck

Last Call

Heart's Desire

The Sweetest Hours

The Big Shuffle

Best Bet

Fool's Mate

Children's

Unplugged

Ava's Adventure

LauraPedersenBooks.com

For Peder Hjalmar Pedersen (1902–1990)
Immigrant, waiter, and practical joker

> *I too walk'd the streets of Manhattan island,*
> *and bathed in the waters around it*
> *– "Crossing Brooklyn Ferry"*
> by Walt Whitman

and

John Anders Pedersen (1931–2013)
Troubadour, humanist, and a real New York character

> *And I will never dread the day I will die*
> *'Cause my sunset is somebody's morning sky*
> *– "My Battle"*
> by Woody Guthrie

CONTENTS

INTRODUCTION

In 1923 my Danish grandfather was working as a kitchen assistant aboard a ship that docked in Hoboken, New Jersey, when he decided to jump off and try his luck in New York City. It was the Golden Age of Ocean Liners, Baseball, and Excess, when liquor flowed freely, despite Prohibition, and Scott and Zelda Fitzgerald adored the Plaza Hotel. They drank there, dined there, and even cavorted fully clothed in the Pulitzer Fountain out front one wild night. Dorothy Parker was cracking wise over at the Algonquin Round Table, a cultural explosion that would become known as the Harlem Renaissance was flourishing uptown, and a flock of Southdown sheep grazed in Central Park. Within a day, Grandpa had a job at a popular Scandinavian smorgasbord restaurant.

My father was born a few blocks from the George Washington Bridge in 1931 and grew up in Manhattan during the Golden Age of Comic Books, Radio Serials, and Skyscrapers, when the Battle for the Heights played out between the Bank of Manhattan and the Chrysler Building, only to be eclipsed by the Empire State Building. (New Yorkers called it the "Empty State Building" since it wouldn't turn a profit for twenty years.) It was the Depression, and the family frequented Horn & Hardart automats, which dispensed sandwiches, baked beans, pie, and even hot beverages to millions of customers cheaply and efficiently. He was thrilled to read the first Superman and Batman comic books, which were set in Metropolis and Gotham, both modeled on Manhattan, and listen to the adventures of the Shadow and the Green Hornet on the radio. Later, when my father went into the army, his mom tidied up his room and threw away all the first edition comics.

After fighting in the Korean War and attending college in Manhattan on the GI Bill, Dad took a job as a court reporter in Buffalo. So I was raised in Western New York during the Golden Age of Serial Killers, Skyjackings, and Disaster Films. It was also the age of steel factories and auto plants packing up and moving overseas. By the time high school commencement rolled around, the local unemployment rate was a whopping 12 percent. Thousands of people would show up for a single job opening, and, all things being unequal, men usually awarded them to other men since they were considered to be "the breadwinners."

The dilapidated War Memorial baseball stadium featured Unemployment Nights during which the jobless hordes made use of discounted tickets to cheer on the minor league Buffalo Bisons baseball team. Meantime, the Buffalo Philharmonic Orchestra campaigned to be adopted by another city. A first. No takers. Bethlehem Steel, that polestar of American manufacturing, imposed a final round of layoffs and then raised an upside-down American flag out front, the international signal of distress. Holy smokestacks! A billboard near city hall asked, "Will the Last Worker Out of Western New York Please Turn Out the Light?"

As 1983 drew to a close, I departed a city with a high suicide rate for one with an even higher homicide rate by hopping a Greyhound bus to Manhattan. People said I was crazy. Why trade blizzards and breadlines for garbage strikes and gangbangers? New York was the dystopian hellscape of *Death Wish*, *Midnight Cowboy*, *Mean Streets*, *Taxi Driver*, *The French Connection*, *Network*, *Dog Day Afternoon*, *Serpico*, *Saturday Night Fever*, *Looking for Mr. Goodbar*, *Superfly*, *The Godfather Part I and Part II*, *The Warriors*, *Last Exit to Brooklyn*, *Fort Apache the Bronx*, and *The Taking of Pelham One Two Three*. In *Annie Hall* an actor explains that he moved from New York to Los Angeles because he did Shakespeare in the Park and got mugged. It was a far cry from the sublime, exhilarating, wholesome 1940s New York of *On the Town*. Or even the 1950s New York of *West Side Story*, where rival gangs displayed their ferocity through balletic dance moves and kick-ass finger snapping. New York's nickname of "Fun City" had recently been changed to "Fear City."

It was a hotbed of arsonists, muggers, rapists, looters, flesh peddlers, flimflammers, purse snatchers, carjackers, streetwalkers, glue sniffers, speed freaks, anarchists, junkies, mobsters, chain grabbers, chop shops, disco queens, dope peddlers, porn stars, Peeping Toms, cross-dressers, jazz hounds, ad men, union goons, radical feminists, atonal composers, street gangs, bag ladies, Bowery bums, Black Panthers, black beauties, bad trips, dime bags, damn Yankees, Hare Krishnas, Hells Angels, angry prophets, crooked cops, punk rockers, psychic stockbrokers, and laid-off dockworkers; a rogue island disintegrating amidst heat waves, killer smog, gaping potholes, collapsing highways, lead paint, racial tension, ethnic warfare, political terrorism, payoffs, gunplay, sirens, slums, brothels, bathhouses, drug dens, bomb blasts, switchblades, cockfights, crack corners, bankruptcy, corruption, roaches, rodents, pigeons, graffiti, litter, and decay. New York had made international news with a near-bankruptcy, a world famous serial killer, a notorious garbage strike, multiple incidents of police brutality, and a citywide blackout followed by riots.

The city was in its late-middle-age Elizabeth Taylor period – formerly glamorous but now broke, bloated, and drug-addicted, with only her diehard fans remaining. It was impossible to know if the Babylonian Burg, with its social contract under siege, was in a death spiral or hitting rock bottom prior to the greatest comeback in history. Much like Liz's followers, residents couldn't tell if they were going to get White Diamonds and Sapphires or Black Death and lemons.

I found an entry-level job as a data clerk on the trading floor of the American Stock Exchange that paid slightly below the poverty line and signed up for night classes at New York University, which students not so jokingly called New York Unemployment. A full course load cost $8,000 a year. Now tuition is $64,000 a year, which Midwesterners consider particularly outrageous for a school with no football team. (The cost of housing varies since a few students can usually be found living rent free in the Bobst Library.) So I got a terrific deal, right? Not exactly, because it has all vanished from my brain – everything from psychology and reverse psychology to managerial accounting and Mendel's laws. The transitive property of inequality disappeared into thin air, while Isaiah Berlin and the Berlin blockade may have been second cousins for all I know.

However, I clearly remember three decades of effervescent New York life – the illegal sublets, token suckers, squeegee men, storefront-window fortune tellers, subway musicians, sidewalk vendors, messianic street preachers, the Botanical Garden's annual train show, *New York Post* headlines such as HERE WE HO AGAIN (about the sexploits of former Luv Guv Eliot Spitzer), and a musical where the entire cast careened around on roller skates. Then, as if New York needed one more act, the circus would come to town – elephants lumbering through the Queens-Midtown Tunnel at midnight with the garish fluorescent lights bouncing off their gold forehead medallions and trunks proudly swaying, followed by eight ponies, three stiltwalkers, and a Watusi. This being New York, the circus had to pay a toll, but there was no extra charge for the trunks.

Chapter 1

I'll Take Manhattan

As my bus lurched toward the Lincoln Tunnel a sign proclaimed: NO TRUCKS OVER 12' 6". Underneath, in equally large letters, was painted: WE MEAN IT! Obviously I was entering a reckless, self-destructive society that couldn't or, more likely, wouldn't follow the kind of simple direction I'd learned in kindergarten. Back home in Buffalo, when my teacher told us not to eat paste she didn't need to tack on a threat. And upon exiting the Thruway near the house where I grew up it wasn't unusual to see a woman hand her entire purse over to the toll taker if she'd just had her nails done. After the Lincoln Tunnel sign I was half expecting a troll to ask me a riddle before I was allowed to enter the Big Bad City.

Having been raised minutes from the border I probably had more in common with Canadians than your average New Yorker. For instance, we Buffalonians know that if you play goalie they have to pick you for the team. Also, that peeing in a snowsuit to keep warm does *not* work the same way it does in a wetsuit – this will just make you colder and cause no small measure of embarrassment all around. I also knew that nose breathing in winter is better than mouth breathing for staying warm and hydrated. And that if you forget your lock de-icer you have to find a guy to pee in the lock for you. Clearly I was going to need a new skill set in this city of sharp right angles.

Of course, I wasn't the first out-of-towner to arrive in Manhattan with nothing except high hopes. Giovanni da Verrazzano, an Italian explorer and part-time pirate who was working for the French, dropped anchor in 1524. He was met by Native Americans who'd inhabited the area since around 10,000 BC, developing into the Iroquoian and Algonquin cultures. Verrazzano was followed by English explorer Henry Hudson, who was searching for a route to the Orient on behalf of investors from the Netherlands, and staked a land claim in 1609.

A local Lenni Lenape Indian told him the place was called Manna-hata, which is usually translated as "hilly island," albeit another version holds that the name came from a similar Indian word for "place of general inebriation." Eventually the hills would be mostly razed for development, but in its long and flamboyant history the city has certainly never lacked for spirits. That's why there's a famous cocktail called a Manhattan, while no one goes into a bar and orders a Minneapolis, a Des Moines, or a Moline.

The Dutch first settled in the lower part of Manhattan, now known as the Financial District, and it didn't take long for the world's most famous trade to occur. In 1626, Peter Minuit, the director of the Dutch colony, bought Manhattan from the Indians for goods valued at around $24. However, one could just as easily argue that the adroit traders here were the Indians since they didn't believe in land ownership so much as stewardship – and therefore the Europeans were trying to buy something that couldn't be bought in the first place.

Along with the desirable real estate came the magnificent place where the continent met the ocean, and created the world's finest natural harbor. It was blessed with deep channels, sheltered ships from storms by extending inland for seventeen miles, and was rarely clogged with ice or else fogbound.

The colony of New Netherland, with its capital of New Amsterdam located at the southern tip of Manhattan, was exceptional from the start. Its reason for being didn't stem from a search for religious freedom, an escape from political strife, or sons being drafted into the army but rather for the sole purpose of commerce. In fact, it would take eight years before anyone got around to building a church, though not because of any labor or lumber shortages, since several dozen saloons had gone up easily enough.

Originally focused around fur trading, but quickly expanding into agriculture and slave trafficking, commerce continued to trump conscience and political allegiances in the bustling settlement. Thus it also served as a popular haven for pirates, with the infamous Captain William Kidd owning a house on Pearl Street and a pew in Trinity Church. The citizenry was a rowdy polyglot, speaking eighteen different languages and frequenting a profusion of taverns, drinking clubs, and grogshops by the time the British came calling in 1664. Gathered in the harbor were only 450 soldiers aboard four ships, but the 8,000 residents couldn't be bothered with whose face was on their money so long as they were able to keep making it. Director-General Peter Stuyvesant was forced to give up the whole settlement to the British so the locals could go right on farming and trading. Even Stuyvesant's seventeen-year-old son welcomed the English invaders. The Dutch city was soon renamed after the Duke of York, brother to King Charles II.

Old Man Stuyvesant duly packed up and paddled back to Old Netherland to fill out the requisite "loss of colony" paperwork. However, after tidying up his career-ending affairs, Stuyvesant returned to his farm in the colony where he and his family spent their remaining years as full-fledged New Yorkers in the capital of capitalism. In return for his service, New York named the large residential development now located on the site Stuyvesant Town, or "Stuy Town" in local parlance, while Stuyvesant High School is one of the finest public secondary schools in the city, and a neighborhood in Brooklyn is called Stuyvesant Heights.

There were two wars still to come between the locals and their new landlords, but by 1820 New York was the leading port of entry for Europe's exports to America. Its entrepreneurial residents were the first to get cutting-edge ideas and inventions from Europe and capitalize or improve on them. When the Erie Canal opened in 1825, the city became the transfer point for crops and merchandise going between the Midwest and the rest of the East Coast as well as Europe. Soon planters in the South began sending their cotton directly to wholesalers in New York, who would take their commissions and ship it onward to the mills

Chapter 2
ON THE SIDEWALKS OF NEW YORK

My entry point to Manhattan from Buffalo was not the grandiose Grand Central Terminal but rather the grotesque Port Authority, a monolithic bus depot on the West Side in Midtown. This steel and concrete block constructed in the style known as Maximum Security Prison shows up on most lists of the World's Ugliest Buildings, and if somewhere there is indeed an architectural monstrosity slightly uglier, I have yet to see it. That said, the inside was even worse. Imagine an Off Track Betting parlor in the lobby of a flophouse.

I arrived in New York City in January 1984 BC – Before Computerization. At least it was before personal computers had landed in every home, store, and office. Back then computers were large, expensive machines used by universities, corporations, and governments for math problems, credit card authorization, military purposes, and weather forecasting; a far cry from the porn and cat-photo delivery systems we know them as today. Before the Internet and electronic signage, information booths were necessary for getting subway, bus, and train route particulars and track numbers, especially since there never seemed to be any maps in stock. Half-mile-long lines snaked from kiosks staffed by one or two employees who acted not bored but truly annoyed, as if you were keeping them from something much more important, such as finalizing a nuclear arms treaty or decoding the human genome. They were downright surly, and if you didn't understand what was being said, their only concession was to talk louder and faster.

There were no mobile phones affordable to us mere peasants, and the payphone banks at the Port Authority were monopolized by pimps and drug dealers. If you did manage to commandeer one, an intrepid bystander would steal your calling card number and sell it to people who would make several thousand dollars' worth of phone calls to the Caribbean within the next ninety minutes.

A statue of actor Jackie Gleason as Ralph Kramden, the lunch-box-carrying, working-class bus driver from *The Honeymooners*, stands outside the Port Authority to help further set its tone as the place where dreams do indeed come true. I wasn't the first recession refugee seeking self-creation, reinvention, and public service on a national scale, or to become "one singular sensation" as defined by *A Chorus Line*. In fact, I was probably the tenth that day, and it was only noon. There were already enough expatriates from Western New York to start our own enclave called Little Buffalo and set up chicken wing stands. But we economic exiles were prepared to hunker down and prove ourselves. Except for people like my friend Mary, who moved to New York for the express purpose of letting some time elapse in order to clear points off her driver's license.

It was two years after Ronald Reagan had assumed office and declared "Morning in America." One of the government's policies was to release mental patients so they could experience the sunrise first-hand. Cutbacks in social programs flooded the streets with people who were psychiatrically challenged and/or suffering from substance abuse. New York City and especially its public facilities were awash with street people, some with hospital bracelets still visible on their wrists. They were panhandling, muttering to themselves, or just camping out, having set up makeshift open-air studio apartments in vacant lots, parks, church vestibules, empty doorways, atop sidewalk grates, under highway exit ramps, and along the East River seawall and the Hudson River's crumbling piers. A prominent feature of these corrugated card-board hovels was the "I ♥ NY" plastic shopping bag. As it happened, in the city's darkest days a tourism campaign had been launched with this upbeat logo in black letters embracing a bright red heart on a stark white background. In no time, these bags became ubiquitous as the de rigueur luggage of the homeless, and the must-get tourist photo was the raggedy jangling street person in heavily layered clothing pushing a stolen shopping cart that acted as a portable closet, or asleep in a vestibule, clutching the prominently displayed I ♥ NY bag. Perhaps the better slogan would've been "NY: We'll Pick Your Pocket and Steal Your Heart."

Another bit of local color at bus and train stations, street corners, and parks were groups of young people with radiator-size boom boxes break dancing on giant slabs of cardboard. Tourists and commuters with a few minutes until their bus or train departed gathered to watch while an opportunistic pickpocket unrelated to the group worked the crowd. It was impossible not to notice how talented these kids were – hopping, popping, locking, freezing, sliding, and spinning on their heads. This was a far cry from the hokey pokey, chicken dance, and beer barrel polka of my Western New York youth. Hip-hop, with its fast, rhythmic beat and self-expressive stream-of-consciousness rhymes, was rising from the ashes of the South Bronx on its way to taking over the music business and becoming a giant cash cow. I can only hope those gifted performers went along for the ride. One Shawn Carter progressed from dealing drugs in a Brooklyn housing project to captain of the rap industry under the more familiar name Jay Z.

In front of the major transportation centers, a scruffy legion of self-appointed baggage handlers and taxi hailers battled to grab your stuff, shove everything into a cab, and extort a fee. Tourists were unacquainted with the improvisational nature of the system and were pounced upon so swiftly that most had no choice but to go with the flow and produce some change or a dollar bill. Nowadays, when I see professional taxi stands staffed by uniformed workers, I'm reminded that they were forged through brutal entrepreneurship, more than a few robberies, and some inappropriate touching.

Between the problems of the nation and a personal budget gap, I was unable to afford a New York apartment and would need to accept an offer from one of the pimps lurking in Port Authority alcoves to snare runaway girls, or freeload off my retired eighty-one-year-old grandfather in Huntington on Long Island. My silver moon boots,

Chapter 3

A Hole in
the Ground

I'm always stunned to arrive in another city and discover actual upholstery making the public transportation system more homey and comfortable. Instead of being jealous, I humbly accept that we New Yorkers can't be trusted with anything but molded plastic. You get the subway you deserve.

The first underground subway opened in 1904, almost thirty-five years after the first elevated train line started transporting New Yorkers up and down the West Side between Lower Manhattan and the Bronx. In 1938, when my father was seven, he could ride the subway from his apartment building in Washington Heights to the Museum of Natural History on Central Park West or Professor Heckler's Flea Circus on West 42nd Street. In Times Square he'd watch comedies starring Charlie Chaplin and westerns featuring Big Boy Williams. The fare was a nickel, a double feature also cost a nickel, and so did a Hershey's bar, as he never failed to remind me during the runaway inflation of the 1970s. No one thought for a moment he was taking his life in his hands by riding the subway alone, nor did the police bring my grandmother in for questioning.

Dad also regularly rode the elevated railway ("the El"), which loomed above Third Avenue. This monstrosity of rusting girders, columns, tracks, and railings blocked out great patches of sunlight on the pavement below and made real estate much less desirable than that situated a block away on Lexington Avenue. Dad said the trains were noisy, grimy, and shaky like a bad amusement park ride, but the good thing was if you forgot to bring a book it was fun to look into the windows of all the people going about their domestic routines. He liked to imagine himself as Dashiell Hammett's private detective Nick Charles working a case while starring in a radio drama.

The El was demolished (most would say thankfully) in 1955 before Dad had a chance to conclusively solve any crimes, but can still be experienced in all its eyesore glory in dozens of old movies such as *The Lost Weekend* and *On the Bowery*. The only advice Dad gave me upon announcing that I was leaving for the big, bad city was not to fall asleep on the subway because someone would steal my shoes.

When I arrived in Manhattan a token cost 75 cents. So did a slice of pizza. Oddly, the cost of pizza slices and tokens basically rose in tandem for more than a half century, and this law of economics became known as the "Pizza Principle." It was also called "The New York Pizza Connection," which sounds more like a mozzarella laundering operation, but actually has nothing to do with the gang that distributed more than $1 billion of heroin that was smuggled through local pizza parlors and resulted in the 1985 "Pizza Connection Trial." However, while the price of a subway ride has skyrocketed to $2.75, a round of vicious price wars has recently put the $1 slice back on the menu in pizza parlor–heavy areas. No one complains about oil prices in New York, just the cost of subway, bus, and cab fares; tolls for bridges and tunnels; and of course that perennial mainstay, the pizza slice. In Spike Lee's movie *Do the Right Thing* the trouble starts when a pizza parlor customer grumbles about the price of his slice.

By 1983 the entire subway system had been reduced to a labyrinth of subterranean urinals connected by tunnels, and was the preferred operating ground for recently released felons, parole violators, addled veterans, sexual deviants, and homeless people.

Whereas in most cities winter is followed by spring, here signs informed me that it was "Chain Snatching Season" and warned, "Please don't flash a lot of jewelry. Tuck in your chains. Don't flash your bracelets and watches. Turn your rings around so the stones don't show. There are only 3,400 transit police. They can't be everywhere, all the time. If you want to keep it, don't flaunt it." Good to know, thanks. Happy spring to you too.

Stairwells, platforms, token booths, and cars were festooned with graffiti inside and out and from top to bottom including windows, doors, ceilings, floors, rooftops, and route maps. In many ways the spray-painted balloon letters, cartoon figures, and mysterious swirls were a joyous relief to the grimy drabness of a blighted soul-crushing landscape, with this vibrant art filling a void, both situational and spiritual. The platforms had no clocks and took on the surreal timelessness of a coal mine or casino. A sensible design choice, since why would New Yorkers hurrying to catch the subway to work or school in the morning with hands full of bags, briefcases, umbrellas, and lattes need to look at the time anyway?

Light sockets went unfilled in cars, stairwells, and platforms, thereby casting long, dark shadows and creating the perfect ambience for a 3-D horror film. The cars themselves were essentially dumpsters on wheels, every surface sticky from spilled soft drinks and who knew what else. Accidentally touch the bottom of a seat and discover a warehouse of previously enjoyed gum. New subway cars went into service (no wonder our economy was so bad if it was cheaper to have these manufactured in Japan and delivered halfway around the world), but within weeks they looked as apocalyptic as the old ones. The only distinguishing factor was that the new cars had seats with molded plastic indentations for buttocks, only they'd apparently used the standard Asian buttocks as a guide. The more ample American backside needed at least one and a quarter spaces, if not more, so this made seating awkward, in addition to making an entire city already suffering from low self-esteem feel officially fat.

Trash, spilled food, and unconscious people covered the car interiors as well as the stations. In summertime the windows remained open if they weren't broken or else jammed shut, and garbage shrapnel would fly into your eyes like a scene out of Dickensian London. The poorly lit platforms were moldy dungeons where paying riders were regularly assaulted, robbed, panhandled, and generally abused. The whole enterprise looked and smelled like defeat.

When straphanger Bernard Goetz shot some young men he thought were going to mug him and seriously wounded all four, he was found not guilty of all charges except the illegal possession of a firearm, for which he served two-thirds of a one-year sentence. The slender, bespectacled Goetz was swiftly dubbed the Subway Vigilante, and his case helped the NRA make it easier to carry a concealed weapon. Depending on your point of view, this either caused traveling underground to become more dangerous because everyone was carrying a gun, or else much safer because people took into account the fact that everybody was carrying a gun.

There were also "token suckers" who jammed the slots with gum wrappers and then skulked nearby. When potential riders inserted their tokens into turnstiles, they got stuck and had to go complain or try another turnstile. That's when the sucker swiftly appeared out of the gloom like a vampire to lean over and remove the token with a big inhale of breath, commonly known as "the kiss of desperation" and "the most disgusting nonviolent subway crime."

One apprehended token sucker struck back at repulsed onlookers by saying he'd kissed women way worse than a token slot. Sometimes a guy would jam all the token slots and then stand by the gate and let people pass at a discounted rate. They considered themselves to be "small businessmen" and "self-starters," while passengers referred to them as "train trolls." It comes as no surprise that the people most disgruntled by this last ploy were the fare cheaters intent on using token slugs to begin with. For the rest of us, after riding the subway on the cheap there was a good chance of getting a half-price newspaper from some guy who'd emptied a vendor box on the street and was hawking them at the top of the stairs.

Having grown up in a predominantly Catholic neighborhood, I was no stranger to overcrowding. Before seatbelts and lifeguards there was always room for one more kid on the bus or in the pool. In fact, climbing into the station wagon with my friend Mary and her eight siblings was not unlike boarding a pirate ship. And when squeezing us all into the frame for a class photo our Catholic teachers liked to say, "Leave no gaps for the Devil!"

Still, while waiting on a packed subway platform you had to worry about being accidentally or purposely pushed onto the tracks. Forget corporate retreats where your team navigates a mud pit, the subway commute remains a daily trust exercise involving more than 4 million riders you don't know and your mother hasn't met to decide if they'd be a good or bad influence on you.

Down below on the tracks lies the dreaded third rail, which, if so much as touched, will electrocute a person with a quick 625 volts. And yet here were these enormous rats blithely crawling across it, basically in paradise since there were rarely any trash cans on the platforms, leaving riders little choice but to toss their garbage onto the tracks. As for electrocution: It transpires that when the rodents hop on and off the third rail they never touch it and the trackbed simultaneously, therefore not serving as grounding posts the way human limbs would. To see the third rail in action watch MTA inspector Walter Matthau corner subway hijacker Robert Shaw in my dad's favorite movie, *The Taking of Pelham One Two Three*.

At the stations I could see restrooms that had been boarded up years ago as crime scenes or potential crime scenes. Meantime, the ones inside Pennsylvania Station not only hadn't seen a janitor's mop in decades, but were overrun with muggers and live-ins who most likely received their letters from the parole board there. In any case, the complete lack of usable facilities put an extra bounce into everyone's step. Public transportation had become the perfect training ground for New York's number one sport – Extreme Bladder Control.

Still, there was a way to perform the daily ballet between human and machine properly if you knew some basic physics. It's necessary to calculate the area of the entire subway car and make sure your body divides the region equally so you're not closer to any one person than another. Every time passengers get on or off the train, the entire corpus distribution must be recalculated. These frequent remixes cause the aggravated conductor to bark, LET 'EM OUT, LET 'EM OUT! If a bus or subway car is almost empty and you sit next to another passenger, this is considered an invasion of personal space and punishable by a glare, grope, or felony. Same with standing in elevators. For those who always groaned, "Why do we need algebra?" the obvious answer is, "For when there's an uneven number of people in any given space!" However, during rush hour, when commuters are packed so tightly that they can feel the keys in other riders' pockets, such close proximity is perfectly acceptable. Whereas some urbanites live cheek by jowl, New Yorkers live face-in-armpit. It just so happens that playing musical chairs as a child is excellent training for getting a seat on the subway.

Identifying the battle-scarred straphangers was a cinch. They folded their newspaper in quarters lengthwise so it could be held in one hand and scrolled while standing up, and they huddled in stairwells to determine whether an express or local train was arriving next, ready to bolt up or down. They could tell where the doors were going to open on the platform and surmise by how other passengers were dressed who was planning to get off at 42nd Street (fancy types catching trains to Connecticut), thereby making a seat available. The person pushing through the short-tempered masses in the wrong direction, known as a "subway salmon," was no member of their hardcore rank. The pros knew that if you saw a completely empty car on an otherwise packed train you weren't the luckiest or most observant rider in New York, but that it was July and the AC wasn't working, or else slumped inside was a person who'd lost all control over their personal hygiene.

Native New Yorkers know that escalators have a slow lane on the right for standing or walking and an express lane on the left for sprinting or leaping, and heaven forbid you're in the wrong one. An irate man trying to race up the left-hand side of an escalator underneath the Port Authority but was blocked by two idlers turned to me and said, "Do you believe this!" It was midday and the offenders were clearly visitors. They hadn't a clue that they were wholly responsible for incapacitating a city of 8 million. He glanced at his watch and said, "If I didn't have fifteen minutes to catch my bus I'd be shouting at them."

One quickly became proficient in all things subway because it was strictly an observation game. Signs stating what train was going where, when they existed, could be counted on to be wrong. The announcements were unintelligible. More than once I was asked by American tourists what language was being used for the subway broadcasts.

The answer was the language the teacher in Charlie Brown cartoons used: "Whaa wah whah wah." Was the man wearing dirty gloves in August a cat burglar or just wanting to avoid covering himself in newsprint (which didn't adhere as well in the old days)? If a car stopped for no reason and an incoherent explanation was made, which rarely happened since the subway pioneered the "don't ask, don't tell" policy, riders would occasionally make eye contact to see if anyone else had a clue as to what was happening. Track fire? Teenagers wilding? Passenger heart attack? Maniac on the loose? Like most multiple choices tests, there were two equally good guesses about what would happen next. If the train had stopped moving, let out an enormous sigh, and was becoming hot, it was probably going out of service. If it was huffing impatiently then it was most likely turning into an express train, and you needed to decide whether to get out. Along similar lines, tourists often asked where to find the "schedule" for the subway and the answer was (in addition to a huge laugh) that it didn't exist, and if it did, would be pointless anyway.

Then, as now, the subway served a dual purpose. It's a low-cost mass transportation system in addition to being a free health-care information center. There are endless advertisements and they change regularly, but you won't see any for yachts, diamonds, champagne, beluga, Armani, or dude ranches. No, these ads are for treating hemorrhoids, corns, warts, bunions, diabetes, torn earlobes, unsightly rashes, acne, nail fungus, hepatitis, and sexually transmitted diseases. It's particularly disturbing to read "Chances are 1 in 4 you will get Herpes" when you're the only one in the car. Visitors would have to think twice about becoming intimate with a New Yorker after seeing these never-ending banners proclaiming our festering, untreated maladies. This in itself cuts down on the transmission of infectious diseases, and it makes one wonder why the Centers for Disease Control and Prevention are in Atlanta and not Grand Central Terminal. The New York Lottery has appropriately chosen to advertise amidst all these cautionary tales and features their tagline, "Hey, you never know."

Eventually, I came to know the subway system and all of its quirks. As I darted down the stairs at my local station I knew the exact number of people I hoped to see standing on the platform, signifying that a train was just about to rumble into the station, and they'd done all of the waiting for me. Less than that and it meant sweating in the gloaming and breathing foul air while hoping for a train with its endless screech of ear-piercing brakes to miraculously appear. More people than the magic number meant that something was wrong and the train could be delayed interminably. This was decades before electronic signs (aka, "countdown clocks") displaying train status removed the excitement of rudimentary prognostication – straining to see around the corners of dark tunnels in search of the glow of a headlight, listening for a rumbling noise, and feeling the ground for a vibration. We were in a state of constant anticipation – what the Boy Scouts, or in our case Homeland Security, might call "high alert." Insiders dubbed the Lexington Avenue line the Muggers Express, the F the Forever train because of long wait times, and the N/R line the Never/Rarely.

In thirty years of riding the subway rails I've never once experienced what the New York penal code calls "forcible touching" in a crowded car. This may just be a statement about my particular body type because I've heard from women who have encountered grinders, grabbers, squeezers, and pinchers. My only observation is that this seems like a dumb move on the part of the groper since he is trapped in a small space, and if the gropee calls attention to the problem there are sure to be a number of people wearing sharp-heeled shoes who will feel obliged to step in and remedy the situation. In other words, hell hath no fury liked a subway car full of New York women who worked a long, hard day in an office, school, restaurant, or hospital.

You aren't considered officially old at any particular age in the city, even though senior transportation discounts kick in at sixty-five. However, it's customary to give up seats to the elderly, and that's when we know we're old. The first time this happens to New Yorkers they all go home and say the exact same thing: "You'll never *believe* what happened to me today!" Conversely, it can be a tough call as to when to offer up your seat. Between cosmetic surgery, chemical peels, and Botox injections, it's impossible to tell the approximate age of many riders. And I've seen more than a few passengers turn hostile when accused of being senior citizens. A friend of mine likes to offer certain women seats "just to see the look on her facelift."

Once I was on a crowded train with a man who had a child about the age of five. (Kids under forty-four inches tall ride the subway for free.) He and his daughter were sitting next to each other when an oversize older woman loudly informed him, "You need to keep that child on your lap since you didn't pay for her to ride." The man shot back, "You should only get half a seat since you paid half price." It's not the comebacks I love about New York so much as that people have them in the moment. I, on the other hand, always think of my oh-so-clever rejoinder about two weeks later while taking out the trash.

A terrific idea for absorbing the continuous congestion would be another subway line. Oh wait – this idea actually occurred to city planners a century ago, and in 1920 a Second Avenue subway was mapped out by a group of engineers who are all dead now. After a few delays because of the Great Depression and World War II, ground was finally broken in 1972 by a team of sandhogs who are also dead or long since retired. As of 2015 the first segment was still under construction. So if you are old enough to remember Ronald Reagan this subway won't be finished in your lifetime. For anyone who ever said that New Yorkers don't like children, let the record show that we *love* children and are inconvenienced daily in the centuries-long building of an entire subway line for our children, or more likely, our great-grandchildren. I don't want to sound pessimistic, but China has been completing subways of similar length within the space of a year, even when hosting the Olympics between transportation projects. In 2000 Shanghai had one subway line and lots of rickshaws. In 2015 Shanghai had twelve new subway lines and no rickshaws. In 2015, New York hadn't had a new subway line for 60 years, but we're getting more rickshaws every day.

To expedite subway construction, perhaps it's possible to raise money by creating first class cars outfitted with Barcaloungers and butlers who offer mimosas in the morning and Big Appletinis in the afternoon, and then wake you in time for your stop. Barbers, manicurists, psychiatrists, tech repair people, and newspaper page-turners would be available round the clock.

The New York subway system is known for its variety, so it should come as no surprise that animals are part of the multi-culti subterranean scene. I believe they're allowed since I've witnessed plenty of cats, dogs, and geckos on their way to the vet or being transferred as a result of post-breakup joint-custody arrangements. And sometimes you see owners returning from the animal hospital with an empty leash or carrier and a tear in their eye, grieving privately in public. Condolences from strangers are proffered. Most of us have been there.

Pigeons and rats regularly make their way onto subway cars, along with a few raccoons and at least one opossum. Dad liked telling the story of an off-duty police officer who was attacked by a penguin while riding the subway back in the 1960s. The rogue bird was returned to its home at the Coney Island Aquarium, but only after five squad cars with sirens blaring came screeching to a halt at the 18th Avenue Station in Brooklyn as they responded to an "officer in distress" call.

During the Discovery Channel's 2013 Shark Week, a three-foot-long dead shark was spotted on a Queens-bound N train. After reports of the car "smelling extremely fishy," a supervisor disposed of the catch-of-the-day, though not before New Yorkers had a chance to post pictures of the shark in various poses, including smoking a cigarette alongside a MetroCard and a can of Red Bull. In the summer of 2013 two subway lines had to be shut down for several hours after a pair of kittens escaped. It was during a mayoral election, and the candidates were immediately asked to take a stand on whether service should've been halted for a kitten search-and-rescue mission. Leave it to say the Anti-Kitten Candidate was beaten in a landslide. (Lesson learned: Much like abortion and taxes, cats also attract a large number of single-issue voters.)

Despite overcrowding and crippling debt, the subway and its environs are now a safe, fairly clean, well-lit place where people read, apply makeup, play video games, and listen to music through headphones. Platform graffiti has been replaced by licensed advertising, which is more uniform and easier to remove, but not necessarily more interesting. Otherwise, the city commissioned permanent mosaics in more than 300 subway stations that are truly spectacular and tour-worthy. A guide can be found online under "Arts for Transit and Urban Design." Another art form called "hitting" has also taken the subway by storm of late. This involves young people (I've only spotted men thus far) performing gravity-busting acrobatic routines in the cars, while passengers try to prevent the airborne artists from hitting the bags and packages out of their hands or giving them a black eye. It seems to be the male equivalent to pole dancing and typically begins with the holler, "Ladies and gentlemen, it's showtime!"

In case you suddenly find yourself in need of cheap batteries, toys, churros, or candy bars, there are plenty of illegal hawkers shouting, "Come get it before the cops get it!" Speaking of which, the list of subway improvements does not include any Quiet Cars. Religious literature is available at most express stops, along with handshakes from politicians around election time. Transit Authority–approved performers busk in stations while offering their CDs or DVDs for sale. My guess is the guy playing the plastic buckets has not been approved. Likewise the man dancing a robust tango with a life-size doll whose feet are attached to the tops of his shoes. Itinerant musicians stroll through cars annoying more people than they please, but have been commended for knocking it off when a sleeping baby can be produced. Some mornings you just want to read the chlamydia ads in sleepy silence rather than be roused by a five-piece mariachi band pounding out "Guantanamera" or else a gaggle of Peruvian panpipers playing the best of the Beatles.

Panhandlers loudly proclaim that they're *not stealing* to make a living. To the panhandlers' credit, they tend not to be thieves and usually work the same subway line or street corner to build brand loyalty and a customer base. In fact, I've seen panhandlers make change for $10, $20, and even $50 bills. There's a hilarious video on YouTube called *Panhandler Party* that riffs on all the wacky stories people come up with to elicit handouts.

It's not enough just to beg in a town that's home to big Broadway musicals. You need an act, a gimmick, a trademark. Even if it's just asking tourists trivia questions such as "What's the best nation in the world?" That would be a Do*nation*. I've run across signs that say "Willworkforfood.com," "Will Take Verbal Abuse for $10," "Cut Out the Middle Man," "My Father Was Killed By a Ninja," "Her Lawyer Was Better Than Mine," and "I Need to Buy a Vowel." Specificity is a popular strategy – "Do you have just a nickel?" or "I need $2.95 for a sandwich" or "My spaceship is broken and they have to send the part from Albuquerque which is going to cost $49.50."

Keeping with the intergalactic theme, an ear-shattering saxophonist on the C train wearing pink fuzzy Martian antennae plays for a few painful moments before announcing to trapped passengers, "Give me money and I will stop." Then there was a guy at my stop selling sniffs of women's underwear for 25 cents apiece or three for a dollar, a somewhat counterintuitive pricing model unless it was meant as a comment on the quality of the experience.

It isn't just the inventive signs that serve to make passersby skeptical. I'm certain that I am not the only one who has seen a supposedly blind or wheelchair-bound panhandler leap up and take off when approached by police or other signs of trouble. Disabled mendicants might do better if they could get a certificate to display, the way some vendors and musicians exhibit their licenses.

My only complaint about subway travel is that tablet computers and other such devices have rendered it impossible to tell what people are reading. It was always fun to size up riders based on their choice of newspaper, magazine, or novel. As a writer it was particularly nerve-wracking to come across a straphanger reading a book that I'd written and then have to study his face for the slightest hint of pleasure or loathing. Now, who knows? That interesting looking guy across a crowded car could be perusing *Guns & Ammo*, *House Beautiful*, or *Street Gangs*. So much for reading material as a conversation starter or creep alert. And if you didn't have anything to read it was almost always possible to look at someone else's newspaper or book over their shoulder. I always tried to be polite when I had an over-the-shoulder reader and left ample time before turning each page in the hopes that others would do the same for me.

The ongoing story of the subway is possibly best told through the contents of its Lost & Found. In addition to the usual umbrellas, briefcases, backpacks, eyeglasses, and cell phones there've been live bombs left by forgetful terrorists, an original Salvador Dali, bags full of cash, artificial limbs, abandoned newborns, corpses, diamond rings, and a large refrigerator stuffed with bottles of Arizona iced tea. A severed head was found on the L train in 2012, the lesson there being don't enter a tunnel through an emergency exit, especially while intoxicated.

Still, things have a way of going full circle. When I arrived in New York there were a number of pantsless riders, and you hustled to another car anytime you spotted one. Over the past few years, "No Pants Subway Rides," where thousands of people show up sans slacks for a "celebration of silliness," have become popular. The event has since spread to cities around the globe, in case anyone was doubtful about New York City's continued dominance as a cultural trailblazer.

In the bad old days, many people took the bus because it was safer, even though it was also slower and so packed with senior citizens that it made you feel guilty about not visiting your grandparents. Nowadays, people ask, "Why take the bus instead of the subway?" On buses – the M1 and the M20 in particular – you can get good recommendations for plastic surgeons or cardiologists. You're also able talk on your phone, which you can't do underground because there's little reception and most phones don't work. Conversely, many riders would argue that the reason to take the subway instead of a bus is that screeching brakes, mariachi bands, bucket drummers, and yo-yo hawkers are preferable to the sound of folks yammering away on cell phones about their personal hang-ups, petty grievances, and perceived slights. Although the worst has to be overhearing the constant declarations of coordinates, "I'm just getting onto the bridge!" "We're stopped at 59th and Fifth!" Like everything else in New York, that's about to change as reception is brought to the subways, and soon enough we'll be hearing, "I'm stuck on the F train right before Myrtle Avenue" with an accordion rendition of "Wake Up Little Susie" in the foreground.

Chapter 4

LICENSE
TO THRILL

At the end of the American Revolution, Manhattan did not extend more than ten blocks northward from the Battery. In 1807 Mayor DeWitt Clinton appointed the commission that would shape the city's streets by imposing a grid onto undeveloped land north of Houston Street. By 1860 expansion had reached 42nd Street, by 1880 it had reached 90th Street, and by the new century Manhattan was completely carved into resident-filled blocks. The only way left to go was up. With some innovations in steel structure, elevators, central heating, and electrical plumbing pumps, that's exactly what happened.

No space had been left to park horses and carriages, which would eventually translate into no space for automobiles. As a result, less than one-fifth of New Yorkers own cars. These city dwellers brag about not having cars the way midwesterners brag about having lawnmowers the size of cars. The percentage of New Yorkers who can drive is much lower than the national average, though the percentage that *can't* drive isn't the same as the percentage that *don't* drive.

A "New York Minute" is an instant. Or as comedian Johnny Carson once said, it's the interval between a Manhattan traffic light turning green and the guy behind you honking his horn. In scientific terms this is known as an LHU (light-horn unit) and the equivalent of 1/100 of a second. As a result, New York is one of the few cities where people wear out horns before tires. But as with the origins of the "Big Apple" nickname, I've heard conflicting stories about the "New York Minute," as some insist it's the interlude between the plates hitting the table in a restaurant and the waiter handing you the check.

A New York Minute is different from a New York Moment, which is something that can happen only in New York, such as a married governor who cracks down on prostitution and then resigns for engaging prostitutes and then runs for city comptroller, or a married congressman who resigns over a sexting scandal and then runs for mayor while continuing the sexting under the pseudonym Carlos Danger to attract the Hispanic vote. Before moving his show out of a declining city in the 1970s, Johnny Carson also said, "New York is an exciting town where something is happening all the time, most of it unsolved."

Statistics show that despite a high rate of cantankerousness and complaining, New Yorkers actually live longer than the average population. This could be based on the New York Minute calculation or else on the fact that when transportation delays are taken into account life just feels longer. If New York City streets are giant arteries, then the cars are the white blood cells, taxis are red blood cells, buses are plaque, UPS/FEDEX trucks are platelets, street sweepers are cholesterol, and garbage trucks are humongous fat globules. Tyrannical bike messengers are the espresso, and Con Edison, which coagulates the avenues from six lanes down to one every few blocks while fixing equipment underground, serves as the mozzarella cheese.

When I arrived in Manhattan, a small number of chunky Checker cabs were still plying the streets, but they had mostly been overtaken by rectangular Chevy Caprices followed by boxy Ford Crown Victorias. Cab drivers were young African Americans, along with some old, heavily Noo Yawk–accented white guys. But I've not seen an American-born cab driver, black or white, in more than twenty-five years. There was a sudden shift to chain-smoking Russians and eastern Europeans who freely offered hangover cures that involved no small amount of vodka and ground pepper, then to Haitians perched on beaded seat covers playing French radio stations, and now to South Asians on multiparty cell phone lines with plates of tikka masala from Curry in a Hurry on the dashboard. In three decades I've had a total of two women cab drivers, and one had her mother riding shotgun in the passenger seat.

Taxis have a thick Plexiglas partition to prevent a passenger from shooting the driver at point blank range. It also ensures that all the air-conditioning remains in the front of the cab while allowing the smell of the driver's dinner to hit you full in the face. If you need a reason to quarry the grimy pleather interior for a seatbelt, it's that the Plexiglas divider six inches from your nose will smash every bone in your face – not *if* the taxi stops short but *when* the taxi stops short. Some riders view this as an avenue for getting free cosmetic surgery and carry a picture of their dream facial features with them at all times since New Yorkers have no single standard for beauty. It's amazing how some folks want their butt fat put in their cheeks, while just as many others want their cheek fat put into their butts.

The current crop of taxi drivers is pleasant and friendly, despite the fact that, while panhandlers can make change in any denomination you want, these cabbies can rarely break a twenty. It is possible to pay by credit card nowadays, as long as the sun isn't shining, in which case you can't see anything on the computer screen. If you're a kibitzer, about one in three of these drivers will tell you they were a doctor in India, Pakistan, or Bangladesh. So now I'm afraid to travel to those countries because if I suddenly need medical attention all the doctors are back here stuck in gridlock. The only real problem with cabbies from the subcontinent is that they learned to drive in a place bedeviled by monsoons and bovines rather than blizzards and black ice, so you really don't want to be their first passenger in a snowstorm. "Turn the wheel into a skid" means nothing to these guys.

I must admit that New York taxi drivers are good about letting ambulances through, not because it's illegal to obstruct the path of an emergency vehicle but because it enables the cabbies to get directly behind the ambulance and pretend to be taking a family member to the hospital. It's possible to see an ambulance with a line of twenty or so taxis and a U-Haul truck following behind, looking as if a Bolly-wood star is being rushed to the emergency room along with most of his extended family. The ultimate game of chicken on the streets of

New York is between NASCAR ambulance drivers and kamikaze bike messengers.

Growing up in Western New York, I knew all about the Pillsbury Doughboy, Michelin Man, Shell Answer Man, and with the bad economy we had more than our share of repo men, but I'd never heard of squeegee men. These tended to be the "working homeless" or "most drug-addled" depending on your reference point, who staked out areas known for gridlock and started washing windshields uninvited. Now, had they actually carried a bucket, scrubber, and cloth, they could've possibly coexisted in harmony with motorists while earning some money, like the unlicensed drivers waiting at airport terminals to take you into the city (or leave you dead in Brownsville) when the taxi line is too long, or the flower and water sellers in front of the bridges and tunnels. But these disheveled practitioners used a corroded sponge and dirty rag to ensure your windshield was grimier than before, demanded money while holding the end of a stick in your face, and delayed traffic. If you thought the carwash was scary when you were little, you should see kids in the backseat being faced down by a squeegee man. That is the real Halloween right there. It's surprising that Stephen King hasn't published *Squeegee Man: Vengeance at the Midtown Tunnel.*

I'd also never heard the word *rubbernecking* until I moved to New York City and the radio blared traffic reports that involved long delays because of "jackknifed tractor-trailers" and "rubbernecking." In Buffalo, one car that had skidded into another was not a novelty worthy of slowing down to gape at. (Also, twenty minutes was considered a long commute back home, and rush hour meant that you went fifty mph instead of sixty.) Furthermore, I knew what "double parking" was from seeing folk stopped outside the post office while they ran inside to mail a letter, but New York City is clearly the birthplace of triple and quadruple parking.

With such traffic density, one might wonder why more commuters don't try to carpool or share taxis. This is because New Yorkers all think they know the best way to go. If you see three New Yorkers get into a car and not argue about the best way to go then a bank robbery has just occurred.

But New Yorkers do generally agree on how to drive, if not the best route to take. Here are a few rules of the road:

1. Always drive through a yellow light and the opening seconds of a red light to avoid being hit from behind. Also, drive through the intersection fast to avoid being cut off and hit from the side.

2. With regard to signaling a turn or lane change, once again we have "don't ask, don't tell." If you warn people that you want to change lanes, they'll just speed up so you can't.

3. There isn't any north and south, just uptown and downtown. East and west are crosstown.

4. Making eye contact revokes your right of way. When no one will make eye contact the car with the most body damage automatically has the right of way.

5. Things in other cities that mean "stop" or "slow down" in New York City mean "go as fast as you can" – for example, sirens, honking horns, yellow lights, bleeping subway doors, and street vendors yelling "check it out."

6. Don't bother looking for speed limit signs. People just go as fast as they can.

7. There's no Main Street in Manhattan. The avenues are clogged enough as it is without designating one as the primary thoroughfare.

8. Crosswalk creep. Drivers waiting for the light to change move as far into the crosswalk as possible so pedestrians must negotiate oncoming traffic or else walk over the hoods of cars.

9. New York City doesn't allow right turns on red. What it has instead are left-hand turns from the far right-hand lane.

10. When driving crosstown don't be surprised to see pedestrians making better time.

To those who complain about the overpriced, overcrowded bridges and tunnels, I've heard these philosophical responses: "It's better than swimming" and "A reason to have good brakes." The Lincoln Tunnel received a big online shout-out from a traveler who declared it "not as infuriating as the Holland Tunnel." On the plus side, you pay a toll only to enter Manhattan. It's free to leave. After a few days here no one has any money left and so the city no longer wants them.

The past three decades you've needed to be a certified etymologist and puzzle expert to understand the 250-word street-parking signs, because to the average driver they look like Sudoku puzzles. There are lawyers, judges, and city officials who specialize in parking. If someone says they work as an interpreter you need to clarify whether it involves the United Nations or parking. Motorists who've been issued parking tickets regularly attempt to employ the defense that the signs are purposely made to confuse drivers. Looking at a parking sign on the streets of New York you could easily mistake it for what we're used to seeing on the wall in an eye doctor's office. This can make the considerably less cryptic signs saying DON'T EVEN THINK OF PARKING HERE! a welcome sight.

In addition to comprehending the signs, one needs to know on which days the alternate-side-of-the-street parking rules are suspended (so vehicles don't need to be moved for the street sweeper), and there are more than forty of them, including the Jewish holidays of Rosh Hashanah, Yom Kippur, Succoth, Shavuot, Purim, Shemini Atzeret, and Simchat Torah; the Asian Lunar New Year; the Hindu festival of Diwali; ten Christian holidays, including the Ascension, All Saints Day, and the Immaculate Conception; and the Muslim holidays of Eid al-Adha and Eid al-Fitr. If you don't have a good memory then mark your calendar!

With regard to incomprehensible parking signs and garbled subway announcements I've often thought: I was born in this state, speak the native tongue, scored well on the reading comprehension section of the SAT, received a National Honor Society Scholarship to college, and I can't understand one word of this. What chance does someone from Buenos Aires or Zimbabwe have? Although one can make a case that oftentimes it's preferable to be in the dark. Bus announcements are perfectly clear and at regular intervals state, "Bus operators are protected by New York State Law. Assaulting a bus driver is a felony."

I've known outlaw parkers who carry garbage cans with holes cut in the bottom and place them atop fire hydrants. To be fair, about one-quarter of the city's hydrants have been defunct since the 1980s and '90s yet remained in place a decade or two later. Some drivers enlist another person to stand in an empty parking spot until they arrive in the same way they get someone to stand in line for them at the DMV or for Shakespeare in the Park tickets. I have friends who have spent the equivalent of weeks sitting in their cars reading newspapers while waiting for the street sweeper to pass or the metered parking period to end. (It was considerably more punishing before electronic devices made phone calls and video games possible.) The newspaper was a signal to other parking-place hunters that, "No, I'm not leaving, *I'm waiting*, so don't bother asking." New York author Calvin Trillin captured the thrill of the park in his novel *Tepper Isn't Going Out*, possibly the only literary entry in the "parking genre."

In an episode of *Seinfeld* called "The Alternate Side," George Costanza causes gridlock, interrupts a movie shoot, and prevents an ambulance from reaching an unconscious man, while he moves cars from one side of the street to the other. In another episode, our problem parker George stops before backing into a space to pontificate on what a terrific parallel parker he is, while another guy starts driving into the space front first and a never-ending altercation ensues over the rightful ownership of the spot. Regarding the limited inventory of spaces and resulting tight squeezes, if you can parallel park it here, you can parallel park it anywhere. Forget singing-and-dancing TV talent contests and truckers who drive on icy roads, we're eagerly awaiting *Parkers of New York*.

The *worst job* in New York City has to be the production assistant whose task it is to find and reserve parking spaces for the many trailers and trucks needed for the zillions of commercials, television shows, and movies being shot every day. This poor person is directly between the New Yorker and his or her parking spot, subject to being cursed at in every language, spat upon, and even threatened with hot coffee or a tire iron.

The Department of Transportation recently announced that they're overhauling the parking signs to "make people less crazy." There's a Catch-22 about the whole enterprise: Any driver believing himself sane enough to understand parking in New York must be insane to want to try and park there in the first place.

On the subject of less or more crazy, thousands of pedestrian-operated push buttons to speed light changes at intersections were deactivated in the 1970s and yet purposely remain in place so that New Yorkers can feel participatory and manage their frustration. Similarly, Manhattan is supposed to be the walking capital of the world with its easy-to-navigate grid and pedestrian-friendly spaces; however, most of the traffic lights are set to favor automobiles and halt foot travelers at every corner.

A true walking utopia would regulate the sidewalks like highways with a fast lane on the outside for regular New York speed walkers and a slow lane on the inside for shoppers, window gawkers, tourists, the inebriated, and folks with dogs, strollers, and small children. Uptown travelers on one side of the street, downtown on the other. Stopping short needs to be punishable by fines and imprisonment. Suddenly coming to a halt on a city street can cause a twenty-person pileup with coffee and pizza slices splattered everywhere.

Tourists might take a tip from the whimsical New York children's rhyme "Cross at green, not in-between, cross at red, and you'll be dead," but the fact is that everyone in New York jaywalks. This is the best way to navigate traffic because you're required to use all of your senses and not follow the directives of a machine. Or as Ratso Rizzo defiantly proclaims in *Midnight Cowboy*: "Hey! I'm walkin' here!" Old folks leaning on canes jaywalk. People pushing children in strollers jaywalk. Dog walkers jaywalk. Seeing eye dogs leading blind people jaywalk. Even the cops jaywalk. Add to that jay jogging, jay biking, jay Rollerblading, and jay skateboarding. Whereas in the Bible "the quick and the dead" means those who sin will be judged by Jesus Christ whether they are alive (quick) or in the afterlife (dead), in New York the phrase just means quick or dead. A populace regularly celebrated for its quick wit and sarcasm should actually be renowned for its quick reflexes and near misses.

Jaywalking in this city is considered an art form, like subway "pre-walking," where you stroll to the exact spot on the platform to board the car that will save you the most time upon exiting. I'm always stunned when I visit European cities and see locals waiting at lights with no traffic in sight. Once when I received a ticket for jaywalking in San Diego I thought I was being punked and looked around for a camera.

I guess that technically it's illegal in New York too, but then so is riding a bike on the sidewalk and I don't see anyone getting a ticket for that. Still, jaywalking is not what kills people in this city, it's texting while walking. If you glance out of a window at night the columns of pedestrians crossing at every street corner with faces buried in glowing phones appear to be one long candlelight procession.

A few years back, crosswalk signals with WALK spelled in white and DON'T WALK illuminated in red were replaced with ones based on the international version of a white man walking and a red hand indicating "stop." No matter the version, it's common knowledge that the fastest way to die is by paying attention to these signs. Aside from these new signs being a statement on the decline of literacy, New Yorkers can no longer say, "I'll meet you at the corner of Walk and Don't Walk." Well, you could, but you'd be dating yourself, like the people who still call the MetLife building above Grand Central the Pan Am Building. Old-timers like my father, who persisted in saying he was off to see "a talkie at the Nickelodeon" well into the 1990s, continued to refer to JFK Airport as Idlewild a half century after the name had been changed. And really ancient New Yorkers, like my grandfather, could recall when men gave up their bus and subway seats to women.

The new WALK/DON'T WALK signs are also *bright*. Not that New Yorkers ever needed an excuse to wear sunglasses at night, since the sun never sets on the cool, but now they have one. I'm not sure if a pedestrian is more likely to be hit by a car due to temporary blindness than if there were no sign at all. When flying up from Florida you start seeing the blazing signals dotting the island from around Harrisburg, Pennsylvania, just before the Empire State Building comes into view.

When my dad was young there were no WALK/DON'T WALK signs, nor were there yellow lights – they just went directly from red to green. Apparently, pedestrians were skinnier, smarter, and more agile back then. They didn't need a countdown clock to determine whether they could make it across a street. Still, though dexterity and personal responsibility have been lost, a sense of humor survives. Young people like to partially tape over the red hand signs so they're giving pedestrians the finger.

Most New Yorkers remain philosophical about transportation delays and are comfortable with the fact that oftentimes you must travel east in order to go west or uptown to go downtown. It's no coincidence that the novel *Up the Down Staircase* takes place in New York. It's a city full of surprise and mystery, the surprise being that you arrived at your destination at all and the mystery being how you eventually got there.

Chapter 5

RENTAL
ILLNESS

When people say, "It's a nice place to visit, but I wouldn't want to live there," they are usually talking about New York. Despite having the highest violent crime rate in the nation when I arrived, New York also had the highest cost of living. A tiny apartment could easily devour more than half of one's salary, and so, unable to afford the skyscraper high rents, I'd moved in with my grandfather on Long Island. Commuting meant rising around 3:30 a.m., getting a ride to the train station, catching the Long Island Rail Road to Pennsylvania Station, taking a subway to Wall Street, then another subway to New York University in Greenwich Village, another subway back to Penn Station, the train to Huntington, and a taxi back to the apartment at about 11:30 p.m. If you've ever wondered about people who can sleep anywhere, even standing up, this is one way of learning how to do it. Thank goodness Huntington was at the end of the line since more than once I awoke in the train yard.

Pennsylvania Station is between Seventh and Eighth Avenues and 31st and 33rd Streets in Midtown Manhattan and directly below Madison Square Garden, which is home to the New York Rangers and the New York Knicks. Manhattan seems to go through Madison Square Gardens the way Donald Trump goes through wives. The first two venues (1879 and 1890) were located on Madison Square on East 26th Street and Madison Avenue. The second MSG was designed by architect Stanford White's famous New York firm McKim, Mead and

White, and the place where – even more famously – White was fatally shot by millionaire Harry K. Thaw in 1906 over his affair with Thaw's wife, actress Evelyn Nesbit. This occasioned what reporters of the day dubbed "The Trial of the Century" and also became a big booster for the insanity defense. The third MSG was an indoor arena located on Eighth Avenue between 49th and 50th Streets that opened in 1925 and closed in 1968.

The Penn Station that my father and grandfather enjoyed was also built by McKim, Mead and White (though Stanford White was no longer with them for reasons previously discussed) and completed in 1910. With its soaring pink granite interior, classical Greek Doric columns, and glorious angel and eagle statues, this colossus was a masterpiece of the Beaux-Arts style and made for a breathtaking entrance to New York City. The main waiting room approximated the scale of St. Peter's nave in Rome and was the largest indoor space in the entire city.

However, the owners decided they'd make more money with a sports stadium and office complex at the location, and thus what was considered to be an architectural jewel of New York met with bulldozers in the 1960s only to be replaced by an ugly, poorly lit, low-ceilinged, completely underground station with all the charm of a stovepipe factory in an architectural style best described as rabbit warren meets Walmart. Similarly, the accompanying office buildings are completely without character, while the fourth Madison Square Garden remains a hideous concrete slab. Much the way Love Canal became the poster child for environmental disaster, the destruction of Penn Station turned out to be an object lesson in historic preservation. It was no coincidence that the New York City Landmarks Preservation Commission was created the following year.

When I'd been a dreamy high school student watching the movie *Fame* about a group of New York City teenagers hoping to hit the big time, there was no mention of living expenses. Upon starting work at the stock exchange I told everyone I met that I was in the market for a cheap place to live. Yes, I was willing to share with total strangers, disregard empty crack vials, feed somebody's python, or do housekeeping.

Every Wednesday morning I scoured the apartment ads in *The Village Voice* the minute it hit the newsstand. Other eager apartment seekers gathered around waiting for the bundle to be unwrapped. Back in the days of paid-for dead-tree newspaper ads, the customer was charged by the amount of space used, and brevity was therefore a money saver. Thus a vernacular had sprung up around the rental market, and it wasn't unusual to see: Bet. Nolita and E Ch Reno Jr. 4 DM DW EIK WIK NR 123 M11. Translation: Between North of Little Italy and East Chelsea a recently renovated one-bedroom apartment in a doorman building with a dishwasher, eat-in kitchen and walk-in closet that has or can be converted to a two-bedroom near the 1, 2, and 3 subway lines and the M11 bus line.

Many advertisements still feature "living spaces" to make it clear that you don't get a house, apartment, or room but merely a place to lie down and plug in a hotplate. A "studio apartment" is a euphemism for a "no-bedroom apartment." And when it comes to a "doorman building," there are two kinds. The first means there's someone in the lobby to approve who is coming and going, collect packages, and generally assist tenants. As for the second, there's a guy who sleeps in the doorway. I was searching for the latter. It's been said that the most shocking thing about the 1975 novel *Looking For Mr. Goodbar*, which was based on a true story and made into a film, is not that a young woman who liked to cruise bars got her head bashed in but that a schoolteacher could afford to live alone in a doorman building on the Upper East Side.

All this doesn't even begin to parse the differences between a condo, co-op, and condo-op. Rather than offer microeconomics at New York University they should've given a class in real estate semantics. It didn't take long to learn that a block with pot dealers was more expensive than a block infested with crack dealers. This was a time when no matter how good someone was at a job you avoided saying, "He's a crack salesman." A "heroin block" was considered luxury real estate to which I could only aspire. *The Village Voice* listed some interesting cohabitation situations, but most cost more than I could afford, and the rest were already taken by the time I arrived, including the one involving leather chaps.

Meantime, I was a swing-shift zombie being kept alive on Snickers bars and DayQuil, until one day I heard these five magic words: *Double-illegal rent-controlled sublet.* A friend from Huntington knew about an apartment near New York University that was only $50 more than my commuting costs and better yet, was replete with all the intrigue and derring-do of a John le Carré novel.

My friend knew someone who'd illegally rented a small studio apartment from someone who had officially leased the apartment, but the subtenant was suddenly off to Athens for a year and didn't want to lose control of the space. Thus was my introduction to "rent control," a practice adopted by a number of large cities in response to World War–II housing shortages that made apartments available at about half the market rate. The actual rules are more complicated than the entire tax code, and I only understood one thing about them: If you weren't the original leaseholder then you didn't want the building owner to know you existed, and since most owners had a superintendent manage their property in exchange for an on-site apartment, then the super couldn't know about you either.

Upon being told the apartment would be gone in a few hours, sight unseen I paid the deposit and first month's rent by handing a cash-stuffed envelope to my friend on a platform at Penn Station. All that was missing was a spy in a trench coat peering around the corner, the sound of a train whistle, and a cloud of smoke, but steam engines had been banned back in 1908.

Fortunately, my new home turned out to be on charming, tree-lined Jones Street in the groovy West Village, across from the romantic European-style Caffe Vivaldi, where Camus-carrying grad students sipped espresso correttos and argued about the influence of Weimar Classicism on Postcolonial theory. A street preacher worked one corner, while a palm reader had set up shop on the other in case one needed an additional point of view. It was a mere ten-minute subway ride to work, a five-minute walk to NYU, and a two-minute trip to the famous John's Pizzeria on Bleecker Street. I could drift around the corner to Bagels on the Square and order a "poppy with a schmear" or an "everything with nothing" and had to be taken seriously, though people still laughed at my thick Western New York accent, also known as irritable vowel syndrome, which made words like "berry" rhyme with "dairy." Across from the bagel place was a McDonald's where coke fiends hoarded the free tiny plastic coffee spoons. Strictly low budget – the guys on Wall Street had tiny spoons made of gold hanging around their necks the way others adorned themselves with Italian horns, Celtic crosses, or Hebrew chais.

It was before the Internet and so on every utility pole or piece of plywood surrounding a construction site were advertisements for concerts, shows, guitar lessons, typewriter repair, or lost cats glued over the "Post No Bills" stencils. Local philosophers, and there were many, pasted magazines photos of famous Bills such as Bill Murray and Buffalo Bill next to the "Post No Bills" stencils. Another consequence of pre-online shopping was that there were plenty of stores selling drug paraphernalia, pornography, and sex toys. Only the proprietors didn't hide their merchandise in the back or behind a counter the way they did in my city but instead created attention-grabbing window displays.

My second-floor walk-up turned out to be a long, narrow space with white stuccoed walls, golden hardwood floors, and a pretty little fireplace. It came "furnished" with a mattress on the floor, small wooden night table, and 17-inch black-and-white TV with no reception, to which I added a $7 orange-and-yellow-striped plastic beach chair.

I'd been instructed not to leave any garbage for the superintendent to take out since he might rummage through it and find incriminating evidence, such as papers with my name on them. This wasn't really a problem since I was fiscally constrained and much like North Korea, produced little by way of trash. I wasn't allowed to officially change my address or put my name on the metal mailbox, but if people sent me letters they might arrive anyway since carriers were more often guided by apartment number than addressee. New Yorkers were no strangers to aliases. Whereas serial killers were automatically issued sobriquets by the press or police, the Mafia normally came up with their own. Over the years we've had Joey Cupcake, Tony Bagels, Vinnie Carwash, Whack-Whack Indelicto, Anthony "Gaspipe" Casso, and The Oddfather (the bathrobe-wearing Vinnie Gigante's other nickname, besides "The Chin").

The laundry room was also off limits. Just as well since some of my clothing still had name labels leftover from camp. And I couldn't lodge complaints about anything, such as the lack of heat or the crumbling ceiling. As for the fireplace, I was warned not to use it under *any* circumstances, as this would cause the whole building to burn down and possibly the entire block. If I needed an ambulance it was clear that I should phone 911 and tell them to meet me at the corner. On the bright side, I didn't need to purchase renter's insurance because legally I didn't exist, and I never received a notice to appear for jury duty.

Oddly, the phone company, which was AT&T in its previous incarnation as a monolithic monopoly, didn't care whose name was or wasn't on the lease. You could get them to install a phone after spending hours on hold, being given a date three months out, and then waiting for workers who rarely showed up. It's not anything like nowadays when the phone company actually wants your business and will even call you at home during dinner to discuss how to get it. This infamous disservice was immortalized by comedian Lily Tomlin in a 1976 episode of *Saturday Night Live* where she plays Ernestine the telephone operator and says, "Here at the phone company, we handle 84 billion calls a year. Serving everyone from presidents and kings to the scum of the earth. We realize that every so often you can't get an operator, or for no apparent reason your phone goes out of order. Perhaps you get charged for a call you didn't make. We don't care ... Next time you complain about your phone service, why don't you try using two Dixie cups with a string. We don't care. We don't have to. We're the phone company."

The only downside for a friendly Western New Yorker was that double-illegal rent-controlled sublet living had much in common with Stasi-operated postwar East Berlin, and the fear that neighbors might be informing on one another was palpable. I didn't dare greet people in the stairwell, but rather hurried past and tried to appear as if I were visiting a friend, which was a challenge when carrying groceries and a big sack of laundry. Knock-knock. "Hi, it's me! I brought the Ty-D-Bol and those clean clothes you wanted!" Names were never exchanged. No one went near the mailboxes unless the hallway was empty. One guy had lived in the building for over a year by dressing like his dead grandmother every time he went out. If you heard screams and gunshots in the middle of the night you went back to sleep.

The rumor that New Yorkers don't care about their neighbors probably got started as a result of thousands of illegal subletters not wanting to be dispossessed. Unlike natural disasters, which tend to bring communities together, double-illegal sublets keep people apart and create suspicion. As in Stalin's Eastern bloc, residents would suddenly disappear under the cloak of darkness, never to be seen or heard from again.

My mini refrigerator didn't work, and so during the winter I simply put milk on the fire escape, a trick learned from living in Buffalo during the energy crisis, when people used the garage as a walk-in refrigerator for half the year. My mother called the apartment the Mushroom Factory since it was light challenged, but having been raised on the Rust Belt Riviera I wasn't exactly accustomed to basking in sunshine. It was a known fact that modeling scouts regularly went to Western New York to sign tall, thin Polish girls who'd never been exposed to the harmful and dangerous rays of direct sunlight.

One night I locked myself out of the apartment. Not having a spare key or even a phone number for the super, I assumed I'd need to find a locksmith. However, a friendly policeman climbed off his horse and easily pushed the door open with his shoulder. Didn't I feel safe now?

Cooking in my apartment was not an option. Like most New Yorkers, I needed the kitchenette for storing out-of-season clothing, schoolbooks, and my bicycle. Most nights I ate dinner and did my homework at the Jack & Jill diner around the corner on Sixth Avenue, which was run by a group of heavily mustachioed Egyptians, all of whom were trying to find women to marry in order to gain citizenship. Even after turning down several proposals, they were still kind enough to allow me to nurse a blue plate special for several hours and thereby absorb some much-needed free heat and light. I was able to pay them back on Halloween when the place became a madhouse because of its location on the parade route. Having worked as a short-order cook back home at a restaurant across from a drive-in playing *The Rocky Horror Picture Show*, I was prepared to serve excitable costumed hordes. Plus, my job as a clerk on the stock exchange had endowed me with a superpower – the ability to quickly add long strings of numbers in my head. Best of all, when my Wall Street boss happened in and saw me working an evening shift slinging hash and diner slang he felt bad and promptly gave me a raise the next day.

Then came the call. The woman I'd never met was returning from Greece on the first of the month. A sign on a lamppost said a roommate was needed a few blocks away on Barrow Street and the price was right, so I headed over there. My new roommate, Bill, didn't tell me his line of work, though the tools of his trade were a small scale, a large safe, and different-size Baggies. He came and went at all hours. My "room" was a kitchenette with a mattress on the floor. I needed ramparts of boric acid around the "bed" to keep the roaches away, much of which ended up between the sheets and acted as itching powder, or maybe more like burning powder.

The guys at the diner had a friend who was owed a favor by the landlord of a nearby apartment and could get me in with an under-the-table payment of $500 cash in "key money." This is different from a "deposit" in that there's no receipt and you never see the cash again. As a result, the following month I was snug inside a studio apartment above an Italian restaurant on Carmine Street complete with a *Honeymooners*–style Murphy bed. This time I met the landlord, a man who favored super shiny suits, two-tone shoes, and a black onyx pinky ring. Once again, I didn't dare complain about anything, but no longer did I need to worry about locking myself out. In fact, it wasn't necessary to lock my door at all. It transpired that there were *never* any robberies above Urbino restaurant, which was just down the block from Our Lady of Pompeii Church, aka Our Lady of Perpetual Bingo, where a scene from *The Godfather Part II* was filmed. Apparently the Mafia had a credo, "You don't hit where you eat." Sure, there were gangland–style mob slayings, but those were all prearranged and rarely resulted in collateral damage.

Today, apartment hunting in New York is as challenging as ever and makes reality shows where people struggle to survive on desert islands, catch fish in perilous waters, work as bounty hunters, or eat bugs look like they're on vacation. Manhattan is currently the most expensive place in the country, with Brooklyn a close second. There's only one guarantee – if you do manage to find a place to live, between the listing lies, finder's fees, dissembling brokers, avaricious landlords, extensive reference letters, nonrefundable application fees, renter's insurance, window guard forms, and a money launderer named Sergei, it'll make for a great story to tell the grandchildren or possibly be the first installment of that Great American Web Series you'd been planning to write. Just remember this: Whether trying to get a job, an apartment, or a seat on the subway, New York will always be based on the Survival of the Fastest. That's why locals talk faster than auctioneers hyped up on espresso. Just *try* interrupting – they can go longer than the St. Olaf choir before taking a breath.

Chapter 6

Man (and Woman) in Black

There are no golf courses in Manhattan. People who live there don't need to pay money to wear hideous clothing. We have the fashion industry to take care of that. There's an entire boulevard called Fashion Avenue, which is home to the Fashion Institute of Technology (FIT) on 27th Street, one of the top fashion schools in the world, and passes right through the heart of the Garment District, roughly 34th to 42nd Street between Fifth and Ninth Avenues. The Garment District contains the showrooms of famed designers who make New York an international couture capital, along with approximately 300 clothing factories, and the world-famous Macy's flagship store. Although one could just as easily argue that the city, founded as a fur trading outpost, was one big garment district from the get-go.

Whereas Denmark has Potato Week to commemorate the days that children would take off from school to work in the fields, and Russia has Pancake Week to celebrate the arrival of Lent, New York hosts Fashion Week to establish that all of the clothes in your closet are completely out of date, you can't possibly afford new ones, and even if you could they don't make the latest styles in your size. Residents live in a constant state of fashion frenzy, which can best be described as What if someone's looking at me?/What if no one's looking at me?

The first thing I noticed while making my way through Penn Station in 1983 were the women's projectile shoulder pads. We had them back home, but they were called sofa cushions, life preservers, and football equipment. Also in vogue for working women were tailored pinstripe suits with skirts instead of slacks, starched button-down shirts, and floppy silk bow ties to finish off the power look. As Harrison Ford's character said in 1988's *Working Girl*: "You're the first woman I've seen at one of these damn things that dresses like a woman, not like a woman thinks a man would dress if he was a woman."

When it came to casual wear the city was awash in parachute pants, leg warmers, headbands, and fingerless gloves, which never caught on in Buffalo, but have always been a staple of Manhattan street musicians. Perhaps taking a cue from the hit movie *Big*, fashion was big – big Brooke Shields eyebrows, big hoop earrings, and for rappers, big gold necklaces that wouldn't look out of place on the front gates of a Hollywood mansion. Based on the mantra "The higher the hair, the closer to heaven," we were living in a city of haloed seraphim. Mullets with their long back and short, high front had jumped from the hockey player backwater to a unisex staple on MTV. Your basic style choices were preppy, power broker, heavy metal, or Flashdance.

Nowadays, New Yorkers love their black. You'd think our city anthem would be Johnny Cash's "Man in Black." It can be hard to tell who is winning in school sporting events since so many New York school colors include black. You can always tell it's summer when New Yorkers appear in their black capris, black T-shirts, black pantsuits, black sundresses, black sandals, and black baseball caps. However, all those psychiatrists who say New Yorkers wear black because that's how they feel on the inside couldn't be more wrong. It's because black is slimming, doesn't show the dirt, never goes out of style, and goes with absolutely everything except my particular coloring.

There's no hunting season in Manhattan because with everyone wearing black, it'd be too dangerous. True, people like to say that if you sit down on a bench in New York you will eventually see everything. But, in more than three decades here I've never seen a Smart Car with a gun rack, a pickup truck with a Confederate flag, a baby in a camouflage onesie, or a local wearing a fanny pack (unless he's selling tour bus tickets on a street corner or working as a second-story man). The only flocks, bevies, swarms, troops, and herds we have are of smokers huddled together in front of buildings puffing on cigarettes, but they do look irritable and potentially dangerous when standing outside in the freezing cold, pouring rain, or stifling humidity.

In New York it's possible to wander about in your nightgown or pajamas and not be bothered. In Chelsea it's a fashion statement. On the Upper West Side you're thought to be crazy. On the Upper East Side you're considered eccentric. In the Village you're one of them. And in Little Italy you're going for the insanity defense.

A 1948 noir movie called *The Naked City* and shot on the streets of New York concluded with the now iconic line: "There are eight million stories in the naked city." Well, they weren't kidding. New York is essentially one giant nudist colony. There's no particular beach, establishment, or vacation spot that caters to the clothing-free lifestyle. It's just that people wander around naked in their apartments, and with 8 million residents in various states of undress throughout the day it's hard *not* to see naked New Yorkers unless you're blindfolded. No telescope necessary.

One of my early apartments featured the Ferris wheel from the Feast of San Gennaro turning directly outside all of my windows day and night. Honestly, you just give up after a while and become an accidental peep show. Whether Ferris wheel ticket sales went up or down I'll never know. I wasn't offered a cut of the profits and didn't receive any complaints when the privates went public. Nowadays, most hotels overlooking the one-mile stretch of aerial greenway known as the High Line contain notifications in guests' rooms about the possibility of being observed while engaged in "naked frolicking." Whether these serve as a warning or a suggestion is impossible to say, especially in the already frolicsome Chelsea neighborhood.

Despite a recruitment booth in the heart of Times Square, the armed forces don't have much luck signing up locals. Most of their enlistees are from outside the city and more often than not, out of state. The idea of wearing one outfit every day doesn't appeal to style-conscious New Yorkers. At the Times Square office, four branches of the military (marines, army, navy, and air force) all share one small bathroom, but if you sign up for a tour of duty you get to use the lav for free and that's something to consider. The New York recruiters have a good sense of humor, and if you're an antiwar protester who chains yourself to the flagpole out front, they'll be sure to hand you a business card.

Fashion-forward New York women (and some men) are known for spending the lion's share of their incomes on costly high-heeled shoes and handbags. Exclusive stilettos and slingbacks have starring roles in all of the TV shows shot here. During Fashion Week of 2012 the Museum at the Fashion Institute of Technology launched an exhibit called "Shoe Obsession" that may just as well have been called "Extreme Shoes," with its 18-inch heels and equally lofty price tags. "Killer Heels" was the name of the Brooklyn Museum's recent shoe show, which featured more than 160 radical designs while exploring the torture, pleasure, and power of footwear. It's probably a good thing that a large number of our lesbians avoid heels and purses in favor of combat boots and big-pocketed cargo pants because it balances things out. More important, with the advent of "lesbian chic," denim-on-denim appears here to stay.

The New York Mafia are well known for being fashionmistas. When godfather of the Gambino crime family Paul Castellano (also known as "Big Paulie" and "The Howard Hughes of the Mob") was assassinated in front of Sparks Steak House in 1985, the killers were dressed in white trench coats and black Russian Ushanka hats. Castellano's successor, John Gotti Jr., was known as "The Dapper Don" for his double-breasted Brioni suits, monogrammed shirts, hand-painted silk ties, and Italian loafers with a sheen that could blind a cat. This would all be exchanged for dull prison garb in the 1990s after he was convicted of committing five murders, racketeering, loan-sharking, tax evasion, and several other offenses.

Even garbage collectors have become sassy style icons, handling the trash with class. The Madison Avenue Business Improvement District issued new uniforms to its sanitation crew, replacing droopy gray coveralls with unisuits featuring gold-colored leg zippers. Its new logo has been incorporated into a patch designed by Karim Rashid, an Egyptian-born designer whose work has been exhibited at the Museum of Modern Art and the Cooper-Hewitt, Smithsonian Design Museum.

Unfortunately for all the actresses, celebrities, and models, there's no more slipping out unnoticed for groceries in sweatpants and a T-shirt without any makeup. These days, cameras are everywhere, and it's time to raise your game if you don't want to jeopardize your chances of landing on a best-dressed list. As for those who are slumming, or still stuck in the Earth Shoe Era like me, at the rate that government agencies are spying on us it won't be long before their insecurity cameras record people's wardrobe information and dispatch the Fashion Police, armed with clothing catalogs, color wheels, and websites.

Whenever I see a fashion magazine I think about group photos from ten or twenty years ago in which we all thought we looked marvelous in pastel overalls or day-glo tie-dye MC Hammer pants topped off with feather earrings or a Blossom hat. Now we howl with laughter. It should be called the Elton John Effect. Similarly, I'm reminded of visiting my dad in New Mexico where everyone appeared so cool and stylish in their western wear that I'd excitedly buy red cowboy boots, a hat with a silver conchos, and a turquoise-studded jacket. Arriving back in New York, looking ready to ride in a rodeo and instead boarding the tram to Roosevelt Island, I felt perfectly insane. I suppose I should just consider myself lucky that Dad didn't move to Graceland.

Chapter 7

A HELLUVA TOWN

Throughout the centuries, New York has regularly found itself on the forefront of mass movements to effect social change, and has produced more than its fair share of martyrs, villains, monuments, and legislation. Elizabeth Blackwell, the first woman to receive a medical degree in the United States, opened a Manhattan practice in 1852 despite considerable opposition. Next she founded the New York Infirmary for Indigent Women and Children where women served on the board, executive committee, and as attending physicians.

One could designate New York the Cradle of Feminization – or else Womanhattan since so many women followed in Blackwell's footsteps. There was Emma Goldman, who illegally distributed information about birth control, and Emma Lazarus, who helped establish the Hebrew Technical Institute to provide vocational training to Jewish immigrants and whose sonnet "The New Colossus" ("give me your tired, your poor") appears on the Statue of Liberty pedestal. There was also Grace Hoadley Dodge, a philanthropist who was the main source of funds for Columbia University's Teachers College along with numerous societies to protect and assist women, and Bella Abzug, a founder of the National Women's Political Caucus and one of the first members of Congress to support gay rights. Wall Street certainly had its prejudices, but in 1986 I became one of a handful of women to have a seat on the American Stock Exchange. The men had a palatial marble restroom, complete with an attendant, and conveniently located a few yards from the trading floor entrance. The gals had a three-seater public school–style lavatory downstairs with metal dividers that was originally intended to serve the half dozen women who operated the pneumatic tube system.

Squabbles surrounding chivalry, chauvinism, and sexism continue to this day. A number of double standards still exist. Should men hold doors for women? Carry their parcels? Allow them to exit an elevator first? Let them be rescued first if the Circle Line sinks? If a man speaks rudely to a woman in New York he may be hit with a sexual harassment suit. If a man wants a woman to speak rudely to him it costs approximately $4 per minute.

In the late nineteenth and early twentieth centuries, Greenwich Village had a number of Black and Tan saloons where the races mingled freely and carried on relationships, an activity that could have led to lynching elsewhere in the country. While interracial marriage was not just socially unacceptable in most places but actually illegal throughout the United States, the Village was for the most part a safe haven where interracial couples could openly cohabit. Similarly, as far back as the 1920s Harlem was a place where blacks and whites might drink and dance together in clubs to the music of African American performers such as Louis Armstrong, Sidney Bechet, and Duke Ellington. The rest of America didn't allow blacks and whites to sit together in movie theaters.

But New York City was like most places in that the biggest reforms usually arrived late and in the wake of disaster. *The General Slocum* was a passenger steamboat chartered to take a group of German Americans to a church picnic but caught fire and sank in the East River on June 15, 1904. The fire hoses had been allowed to rot, the lifeboats were inaccessible, and the life preservers were decayed and useless. Of the 1,342 people aboard, an estimated 1,021 died. The disaster resulted not so much in regulations to improve the emergency equipment on passenger ships but in safety inspections (not involving corrupt officials) to make sure the standards already in place were being followed. The Triangle Waist Company fire in Greenwich Village on March 25, 1911, killed 146 garment workers, mostly young women, because management had locked the exit doors and blocked the stairwells. This tragedy resulted in legislation improving factory safety standards, galvanized the International Ladies' Garment Workers' Union in its fight for better working conditions, and gave laborers the support of politicians.

Many more fights were to follow, including those for a woman's right to vote, seek equal pay for equal work, and make decisions about her health care. In 1947 Jackie Robinson would put on a Brooklyn Dodgers uniform (no. 42) and break the color barrier in baseball. Meantime, many locals fought for civil rights at home and by sending citizens down South to protest segregation and sign up voters. New Yorkers Michael Schwerner (age twenty-four) and Andrew Goodman (age twenty) would be shot dead at point blank range along with Mississippian James Earl Chaney (age twenty-one) for their efforts.

Author Tom Wolfe branded the 1980s "The Me Decade," but in New York it just as fittingly could've been called "The HIV Decade." Along with San Francisco, New York City had long been a safer haven for the LGBTQ crowd (before it had letters) than most of the United States. There was the famously tolerant Greenwich Village with its many gay bars and bathhouses on and around Christopher Street, and freewheeling Chelsea, where the McBurney "Y" on West 23rd Street was celebrated in the hit Village People song "Y.M.C.A." All that began to change in 1981 when *The New York Times* announced the discovery of a transmittable "gay cancer" that we've come to know as AIDS. The news continued to grow worse as the paper filled with obituaries of talented men dying in their prime. Suzy Benzinger, my friend from Western New York, and now a Broadway costume designer, had her entire address book wiped out by AIDS. She can't so much as look at a photo album without bursting into tears. By age thirty almost all of her contemporaries were ill or had died.

The city's streets began to fill with protesters wielding *Silence = Death* signs covered in pink triangles, demanding awareness and assistance. With more than one-quarter of all AIDS cases located in New York, it quickly became a hub for fund-raising to provide services for people with HIV/AIDS and find a cure. Help certainly wasn't coming from the top down. President Ronald Reagan, New York mayor Ed "How'm I doin'?" Koch, and religious groups were dismissive. It should've helped that Reagan was a movie star and had close friends like Rock Hudson, the first major celebrity to publicly admit to having AIDS and then die of its complications. It should've helped that cheerleader-in-chief Mayor Koch was most likely a closeted gay man. More than 850 New Yorkers were dead of the disease by the end of 1983, but the Koch administration had spent only $24,000 on AIDS. (That said, Koch did have a pro-gay-rights record when it came to pushing for equality and ending discrimination.) As for the many powerful church groups, it should've helped that Jesus healed the sick and fed the hungry.

An epidemic mindset took over the city, especially when it came to light that anyone could contract AIDS, including straight people, women and children, and drug addicts, though medical professionals weren't yet certain about the specifics. It was announced that you could catch it from a routine blood transfusion. Somebody had contracted AIDS from a trip to the dentist! It was no longer safe to share a toothbrush. People were frightened, and not just with regard to dating. Whenever anyone, gay or straight, caught the flu or lost weight we questioned whether it was AIDS, and coworkers were probably wondering the same about us. A once routine scratchy throat or a canker sore was considered to be a potential death sentence.

In the absence of large-scale government assistance, the public took matters into its own hands by creating grassroots agencies. An enormous number of inventive, determined, and caring "average" gay and straight people helped millions of victims and continue to do so with dozens of organizations, including the AIDS Coalition to Unleash Power (ACT UP), Gay Men's Health Crisis (GMHC), God's Love We Deliver, and Broadway Cares/Equity Fights AIDS.

If one good thing came out of the long horror that was and continues to be the AIDS/HIV crisis, it is that today most people feel they can be honest about their sexuality and not fear being shunned by society. The city and the country now have a number of openly gay politicians, many of whom are married to their partners, and some of whom have divorced their partners and are fighting over property and child custody – like countless other Americans.

In other news, the Queensboro Bridge was renamed in honor of Ed Koch in 2010. Call it poetic justice or perhaps divine retribution.

Chapter 8

Stayin' Alive

FORD TO CITY: DROP DEAD was the famous *Daily News* headline on October 30, 1975, and in the annals of newsprint possibly only topped by the *New York Post*'s HEADLESS BODY IN TOPLESS BAR in 1982, though the *Daily News* got in a good jab with SOMOZA SLAIN BY BAZOOKA in 1980. The way it turned out to be a bad idea for President Lincoln to go to Ford's Theatre, it probably would've been a bad idea for President Ford to go to Lincoln Center that week. The city teetered on the brink of bankruptcy and the federal government wasn't inclined to help, though it eventually provided loans (which were repaid, with interest).

However, one headline credit goes not to a newspaper but to a sportscaster, ABC's Howard Cosell. During the 1977 World Series he cut to a helicopter camera for an overhead view of the neighborhood surrounding Yankee Stadium where an abandoned elementary school was on fire a few blocks away and reportedly announced, "There it is, ladies and gentleman; the Bronx is burning." The Lower East Side of Manhattan was also on fire since landlords there could make more money by burning buildings down rather than fixing them up and renting them out.

The French Connection was a dramatic thriller shot in New York during its glorious gritty phase, and in an online film forum someone recently asked, "Was it all filmed in ghettoes?" No, the movie was made in neighborhoods where people lived and worked, including the supposedly swank Upper East Side of Manhattan, where rats are referred to as rodents. Former Beatle and peace activist John Lennon was shot outside of his Central Park West apartment building on December 10, 1980. The rock star's assailant later claimed he did it to get attention. In his last interview Lennon had said, "Wasn't the seventies a drag? Here we are, let's try to make it through the eighties, you know?"

By the time I arrived in Manhattan, everybody had been the victim of some sort of crime. At the stock exchange a colleague's twelve-year-old son had been mugged five times on the way home from school. I'd never even known a young person who'd been the victim of any type of violence unless it involved spitballs or snowballs. When I was sitting in a jury box with two dozen others and we were asked if anyone had ever been mugged, every single hand went up except mine.

Not that crime was anything new to New York City, home of Five Points, a notorious downtown slum that allegedly had the highest murder rate in the world in the nineteenth century. In fact, famous frontier outlaw William H. Bonney, better known throughout the Wild West and in dime novels as Billy the Kid, was born on the Lower East Side of Manhattan in 1859. He even got started by committing his first homicide here. Murder Incorporated was the name the press gave to the hit men who operated as the enforcement arm of the Mafia in the 1930s and '40s, though I'm guessing that despite the professional-sounding name, they weren't listed in the phone book and didn't file tax returns.

As it happens, homicide statistics date all the way back to the week Henry Hudson and his crew dropped anchor in the lower bay of what would become New York Harbor in September 1609. The exploring party's initial contact with the Delaware Indians, who had welcomed Giovanni da Verrazzano eighty-five years earlier, was described as being very friendly. However, four days later, when a small crew returned from exploring the Upper Bay and the Narrows by boat, they were attacked by Delaware braves in a pair of canoes. Two sailors were wounded and one was killed by an arrow through the throat.

What people were experiencing in the 1970s and '80s was a rise in crime from previous decades, especially street violence. New York's murder rate had quadrupled between 1960 and 1975. This was largely the result of a bad economy, the departure of manufacturing jobs, an increased drug trade, and a surge in the homeless population. Of all the heroin addicts in the country it was estimated that more than half were in New York. Meantime, this was no longer the great port city it had been from inception right up through the 1950s, when competing modes of transportation and union troubles caused a sharp decline in shipping.

Not one but two New York baseball teams, the Dodgers and the Giants, bolted for sunny California. Professionals fled to the suburbs, thereby eroding the tax base even further, and it was a downward spiral from there. Those who stayed behind double- and triple-locked their doors while adding steel bars to the windows (even though you couldn't see the people or possessions inside as most windows were covered in grime from factory smoke and car exhaust). Truck drivers refused to make deliveries in certain neighborhoods without police escorts. School kids gave the rats that inhabited their classrooms names. The mighty Hudson River, where my father used to go swimming, had become a toxic dump for industrial contaminants.

So you didn't make eye contact when out on the street, tried not to be alone anywhere, and always kept handy a $20 bill known as "mugger money." You never wanted to make a thief angry by only having a couple of bucks, because if he was in need of a quick fix, being broke was a good way to get killed. Also, if your mugger money was in a purse or wallet then you could put the rest of your cash in a shoe or secret pocket. I knew men who carried decoy wallets in their back pockets filled with expired store coupons and a sarcastic note declaring the felon had been fooled. If people were ever beginning to act a little crazy around you, it could never hurt to start acting crazy yourself and try to out-crazy them with babbling and twitching, the way Paul Newman disarmed his knife-wielding attacker in *Fort Apache the Bronx*. People with visible tattoos were to be avoided as they were either badass ex-marines, gang members, or former felons, not benign students and makers of artisanal okra.

The homegrown Guardian Angels set up shop in 1979 to protect people from violence and crime. These unarmed volunteers in conspicuous red jackets and red berets made citizen's arrests while patrolling the streets and subways. At first the local government rejected the self-appointed superheroes, but then quickly realized it needed all the help it could get.

Defense tactics aside, one still felt sorry for street people and addicts because most were clearly in need of medical attention. But left to their own devices, many had developed a threatening aura, probably in large part by trying to keep from becoming victims themselves. However, my question was this: Why do so many seem to hear voices that tell them to disrupt events or commit violent acts? Where were the voices telling people to work in the community garden, assist the elderly, and return any overdue library books?

Before cell phones, it was easier to identify who was disturbed because they'd be talking to themselves, usually engaged in a heated stream-of-craziness argument. (One could well ask: If you're going to have an imaginary friend, why not choose someone you get along with?) Anyway, since the advent of hands-free phones, everyone now walks around seemingly talking to themselves, looking agitated and insane.

Springtime in New York in the 1980s didn't just mean getting mugged under blossoming cherry trees, it also meant the appearance of "trash twisters" on windy days, a result of all the stray plastic bags that had thawed out, and "floaters" in the East River – those who'd run afoul of gangsters and been sent to "swim with the fishes" but had lost their cement overshoes. Of course, bodies also turned up in car trunks and storage lockers in the bad old days. As everyone knows from watching *Goodfellas*, it can be damn hard to get rid of a body around here. Speaking more poetically, *Spring has sprung, the grass has riz, I wonder where the bodies is?*

New Yorkers became accustomed to a certain amount of crime in the '80s. After all, it's never been lost on us that we have a great deal in common with convicts. New Yorkers eat on the run, wear layers of clothing, can always use a dependable wheelman, and don't make unnecessary polite conversation. Plus there's no shortage of bravery among a people who hop into cars with complete strangers and eat food from pushcarts on the street. There's a reason frankfurters are called "dirty water dogs," or "haggis" if you're Scottish. Then again, New

Yorkers don't have much sympathy for prisoners living in 10 x 20 foot cells with annoying roommates and/or neighbors, compliments of the government, when they're paying $2,200 per month plus utilities for the exact same accommodations.

In my small suburb outside Buffalo, people would leave their cars running with the keys in the ignition while they popped into stores, church, or a friend's house. Once you'd started a rusted-out beater, which is what most of us had amidst the double whammy of bad weather and a bad economy, it was wise not to take chances, especially in wintertime. Folks would start the car in the morning an hour before work and leave it running in the driveway or on the street while they showered and ate breakfast. Not only was this not an option in 1970s and '80s New York City, but drivers there didn't stop at red lights in many neighborhoods for fear the car would be stolen with them inside it.

The decades-long crime spree featured homemade cardboard signs in windshields declaring NO RADIO IN CAR and EVERYTHING ALREADY STOLEN. Dr. William Portnoy's sign should've said HEADHUNTERS ONLY. Portnoy's complaint was that six human heads intended for medical research were stolen from his trunk and then discarded in a gutter after the thief realized there was no secondary market for his plunder.

The main question of 1980s New York: Which was worse, the robberies or the subsequent car alarms that kept an entire city awake as they shrieked the nights away? Racket rage led to alarms being deactivated with bats and guns, which just resulted in more crime. While tourists went around whistling their favorite Broadway show tune, New Yorkers were left humming their favorite car alarm. A mechanically minded friend of mine installed a car alarm that sounded like gunshots. That always got a quick response from the police.

Central Park was overrun by rats, pushers, hustlers, junkies, stabbers, swindlers, thugs, and muggers. Or, as my mother the psychiatric nurse would say, "Persons engaged in a wide spectrum of antisocial behaviors." As for the monuments, benches, bridges, pathways, and railings, they suffered from corrosion, graffiti, vandalism, and neglect. The tunnels served as crime scenes, vagabond living quarters, and public lavatories. The park's lights were burned out and the fixtures smashed, while the "playgrounds" consisted of brown patchy grass littered with discarded hypodermic needles and broken glass. "Grown men come in the park and don't leave alive," was how one of the robbers summed it up in *Home Alone 2: Lost in New York* – a children's movie.

Meantime, Tompkins Square Park in the East Village was operating as a full-blown Hooverville, complete with shanties and trash-can fires that served as a homeless encampment but also a gathering place for drug dealers, skinheads, and other disaffected youth whose main occupation was drinking to excess, playing loud music, and lighting firecrackers. This odd mix of patrons coexisted respectfully until 1988 when resident noise complaints brought about a curfew, which led to riots between police and pretty much everyone else.

In the late 1980s came the harshest blow of all – our sandboxes were taken away. Parks Commissioner Henry J. Stern declared that having sandboxes in parks and playgrounds required a higher level of social responsibility than some of our citizens possessed. Ouch.

Times Square had likewise hit on hard times. In addition to several legitimate Broadway theaters, freewheeling 42nd Street between Seventh and Eighth Avenues was the main drag for dealers, drifters, grifters, users, boozers, hucksters, suckers, strippers, derelicts, doomsayers, fast talkers, cardsharps, cops, pimps, peep shows, seedy bars, clip joints, grindhouses, porn shops, and fleabag hotels, and not coincidentally the block with the highest crime rate in the city. Legions of gum-cracking prostitutes plied the neighborhood in sequined halter tops, hot pants, stiletto-heeled slides, and patchwork rabbit fur jackets.

Two hundred police officers were assigned to the few blocks that made up Times Square, yet they didn't make a dent in the crime rate. An area that in the 1920s had been synonymous with wealth and entertainment; home to upscale hotels, trendy restaurants, and elegant theaters; and iconified as "The Center of the Universe" and "The Crossroads of the World," was now known as "The Cesspool of the World." And "Swing Street," which is what they called West 52nd between Fifth and Sixth Avenues in the 1930s and '40s because of the jazz clubs featuring the era's greatest performers, was now nicknamed "Sleazy-Second Street."

Times Square was also the street scam capital of America. Hustlers have been running three-card monte games in New York since at least the 1870s. More than a century later they were still going strong. In this particular scam, a cardboard box or plastic crate is turned upright, three cards are shown and then shuffled, and then a rube is supposed to bet on the location of one card. ("Watch the red, and around and around it goes, find the red and your money grows, find the black and you don't get nothing back.") If there aren't any suckers the shill bets and wins. If a victim is about to take the bait, the shill urges him on. The house rarely loses, because the dealer is extremely skilled. Most of these swindlers had become proficient in the first place by practicing for hours every day in prison. Resident Times Square raconteur Damon Runyon had warned the wide-eyed visitor to New York City: "One of these days in your travels a guy is going to come up to you and show you a nice brand-new deck of cards on which the seal is not yet broken and this guy is going to offer to bet you that he can make the jack of spades jump out of the deck and squirt cider in your ear. But son, do not bet this man, for as sure as you stand there, you are going to wind up with an earful of cider."

Not as debauched but just as dodgy were Astor Place, gateway to the burned-out crack-infested East Village, and the Bowery (better known as Skid Row), which were home to seven-day-a-week unlicensed and unrestrained riffraff flea markets. Winos and vagrants would rummage through trash for castoffs such as a torn men's flannel shirt, stained sundress, single earring, battered toaster, chipped mug, or old magazine, and set these items out on the pavement for sale. Green-minded citizens should be proud to know that recycling has always existed in Manhattan at some level, going all the way back to the droves of swine that lived off garbage flung into the streets and would eventually become Christmas hams.

As it happened, Mafia-run neighborhoods with their Madonnas on the front lawns were the only places where children could safely play outside and old people could shuffle down the streets without getting robbed. As I mentioned before, there weren't any random muggings or stabbings where I lived on Carmine Street in the Italian section of Greenwich Village; I suspect the butcher shops kept ready-to-serve horse heads frozen in the back. Likewise, Little Italy in Manhattan, Bensonhurst in Brooklyn, Arthur Avenue and Morris Park in the Bronx, and much of Staten Island, in addition to having the best fireworks displays, were considered safe for pedestrians at all hours of the day and night, so long as you weren't the target of an arranged hit or the wrong ethnicity.

Chapter 9

THE TURNAROUND

The FBI tips hotline rarely gets calls from concerned New Yorkers. For one thing, your average resident is more worried about death by bike messenger than a terrorist attack. Second, the directive to report unusual sights and behavior can't exactly be applied here. Between the steaming manholes, performance artists, everyday street drama, naked cowboys, brown-robed Franciscan Friars wearing bright orange Crocs instead of sandals, and people dressed in everything from superhero to cartoon character to chicken costumes, one wouldn't know how to begin to define *unusual*. All of Greenwich Village, Times Square, and the Lower East Side might have to be cordoned off with police tape.

Nobody thought it particularly odd that a 1972 Brooklyn bank heist was embarked upon so that one of the robbers could pay for his male lover's sexual reassignment surgery. The bank job was botched and the robber ended up doing jail time, but he was paid for the rights to his story and 1 percent of the resulting film's net profits, which were used to finance the sexual reassignment surgery so that Ernest could become Elizabeth. The movie, *Dog Day Afternoon*, went on to win an Academy Award for the best original screenplay.

In the meantime, Homeland Security has declared that people who are sweating profusely and not making eye contact are probably terrorists. That's every single New Yorker taking the subway on a sweltering August day.

Strange things are always happening in New York. Poets wander the streets selling verse-on-demand, while people covered in boa constrictors or live parrots offer themselves up for photographs. The fact that there are 8 million people in the city means that when someone says there's a one-in-a-million chance of something happening, it will happen eight times a day in New York. Likewise, it's pretty bad to be called the town drunk in a place with 8 million people. Still, you can be assured that if you visit a place like Denmark, which has 5.6 million people in the entire country, someone will ask if you know so-and-so from New York. I'd find this silly except that when people ask if I know so-and-so from Buffalo, a city of 260,000 people, I almost always do.

Violent crime in New York City finally began to drop in the early 1990s. "Dart Man" seems to have signaled the end of our head-line-grabbing maniac-on-the-loose phase. This particular attacker was shooting darts into the posteriors of women on the street during the summer of 1990, claiming more than fifty victims. People feared his projectiles were laced with poison or the AIDS virus. Since Dart Man's targets tended to be wearing business suits, women around the city immediately ditched their skirts in favor of shorts, leggings, and capri pants. A thirty-three-year-old Bronx resident named Jerome Wright was apprehended by police and identified by three of the woman. Wright was granted bail at $1,000 and the charges were reduced to misdemeanors. That must have taught him a lesson he'll never forget.

Today's scams are rather mild in comparison to the days of darts and manslaughter. People stop you on the street with a long story about how they need money for a train ticket to Westchester, Ronkonkoma, or Plainfield – basically the urban version of begging for gas money. Then you get a few daredevil cyclists who wait for people to enter a bike lane, purposely crash into them, scream how they could've been killed by such stupidity, and proceed to extort money. A similar (but less dangerous) ploy involves finding a deli container with some half-chewed leftovers and a price of about $9.95 on it, collide with a pedestrian staring down at her phone, show her the price of your "food," and extract reimbursement.

Oddly, kidnapping for ransom never took off in New York the way it has in Mexico, Haiti, and the Middle East. Living in such cramped quarters results in a certain amount of bedroom envy that might weigh heavily against a payout. Or maybe it's just too hard to grab someone off the E train and drag him through the turnstile, up two flights of stairs, and into a waiting car that gets stuck in gridlock. Most witnesses would probably just assume it to be some sort of performance art.

The decline in crime has been variously attributed to a larger police force, changes in law enforcement tactics, the end of the crack epidemic, using computerized statistics to map crime, applying the "broken windows" theory (addressing vandalism and fare-beating before it snowballs), the legalization of abortion (controversial), and the decline in lead poisoning among children. The widespread use of electronic payments has also played a role in putting muggers and pickpockets out of business.

A large number of public and private initiatives have helped get people off the streets and into shelters, apartments, and treatment programs over the last three decades. Still, the problem of homelessness is far from resolved, and despite a reduction in the number of visible street dwellers, advocacy groups say there are more people in city-run shelters today than thirty years ago. As the system stands now, it's more rewarding to build high-end apartment buildings that attract a wealthy clientele than to put up affordable or subsidized housing. Meantime, charities and religious organizations feed thousands of people, including children, every day.

Many survivors whine about Times Square being Disneyfied since it's now home to refurbished theaters, theme restaurants, chain stores, and major retailers, in addition to all types of family-friendly entertainment. A host of cartoon and comic book characters roam the area waving, smiling, and offering to pose for pictures with visitors in hope of a tip. (When one of the dozen or so big, bushy, red Elmos broke rank and screamed obscenities at tourists there was a quick intervention and he was packed off to Muppet rehab.) As for the Naked Cowgirl, gravity would suggest that she's more of a Naked Cowgrandmother.

Seriously, people, I realize we're short on space in this city, but was it ever a good idea to combine a Theater District and a Red Light District into a hodgepodge crazy quilt of people seeking opposite types of entertainment all under blazing neon lights and a big zipper? The avant-garde and mostly nude *Oh! Calcutta!* was possibly the only crossover show between the area's two clienteles. It was bad enough when I took an East Harlem school group to see *Oklahoma* and they assumed that the smokehouse was a crack house. Should children really encounter their first mainliner on the day they see their first headliner?

Central Park is now a fairy-tale playground visited by more than 25 million folks a year – second only to Times Square – in large part because of the nonprofit Central Park Conservancy. In this case, I must admit that I do miss being able to relax next to a dope peddler without being run down by another corporate-sponsored marathon or surrounded by throngs of excited bird-watchers. And I find it odd that among the more than two dozen statues in Central Park that commemorate artists, explorers, presidents, and military men, there are none honoring (real) women. Even Balto, the heroic Siberian husky sled dog, is a male. As a consolation prize, there are statues of the imaginary and nonthreatening females Alice in Wonderland and Mother Goose. At least the *Angel of the Waters* sculpture in the park's Bethesda Fountain, which was unveiled in 1873 and had a starring role in *Angels in America*, was designed by a woman. Emma Stebbins became the first female to receive a public commission for a major work of art in New York City, and it clearly didn't hurt that her brother was president of the Central Park Board of Commissioners. An old joke about all these monuments is that a statue of a pigeon should be erected so that generals can come and sit on it.

Tompkins Square Park is likewise a bucolic oasis complete with playground where it's possible for children to run around without stepping on discarded needles. However, when the park hosts a riot anniversary concert, the event can be counted on to produce at least one brawl where the police need to step in.

Much of New York's vast park system has been similarly upgraded, and there are now acres of space to picnic, relax, hike, and kayak.

Prospect Park in Brooklyn, with its rolling hills, immense lake, and ancient trees, has a more tranquil ratio of nature to humans than Central Park. It's a spectacular galvanized jumble of flora, carousel, zoo, and women in burkas throwing a barbecue adjacent to a Ghanaian soccer game across from Mexicans celebrating a quinceañera. The only time to avoid the parks nowadays is right after the New York City Marathon when all the couch potatoes suddenly decide they're gonna be contenders and clog up every woodland trail, outfitted in brand-spanking new sneakers and tracksuits. Fortunately, this rush for fitness lasts only a few days, and then they're all back home with a platter of nachos on their laps, fully engaged in spectator sports such as *Storage Wars* and *The Biggest Loser*.

There are now dozens of community gardens throughout the five boroughs where it's possible to volunteer, exercise your green thumb, and learn to harvest rainwater. Additionally, hundreds of tourist- and marathon-free neighborhood miniparks are safe places where children play, young people strum guitars, seniors cluster together for gossip or dominoes, and a variety of folk come together for games of chess. A regular is most likely feeding pigeons, and the sociable squirrels will eat right out of your hand.

The only threat in city parks nowadays is a new strain of brazen, stand-your-ground raccoon. Members of a theatrical troupe of raccoons living underneath the Delacorte Theater in Central Park revel in making scamper-on appearances during Shakespeare in the Park productions. It must be an acting challenge for Hamlet's mother, Gertrude, to lie dead on stage while a raccoon is tugging at her braid. I believe this profusion of masked bandits may have something to do with the fact that I haven't seen a rabbit in more than ten years, except on dinner plates in French restaurants.

The Hudson River was designated as a cleanup site by the Environmental Protection Agency in 1983, in large part thanks to efforts by folksinger/activist Pete Seeger and PCB archenemy Robert Kennedy Jr. "America's Rhine" is now safe for fishing, jet skiing, windsurfing, and swimming, though the Department of Health recommends that you (1) don't swallow water, (2) consider keeping your face and head out of the water when swimming, and (3) wash your hands after swimming. Oddly, they say nothing about how long you must wait to swim after eating in order to avoid getting a cramp.

The Mafia have all taken jobs as television actors, writers, and consultants. As a result, what we used to be able to watch for free on the streets we must now shell out $15 to see in a movie theater or else subscribe to cable. Meantime, TV shows such as *Seinfeld*, *Friends*, *Will & Grace*, *Sex and the City*, *Felicity*, *Ugly Betty*, *White Collar*, *Girls*, and *Smash* started showing New York as a fashionable and fascinating place to live where excitement in the form of someone wearing expensive shoes or a Soup Nazi is always just around the corner.

New York has declined so far in crime that it didn't even make the most recent list of the 100 Most Dangerous Cities in the United States, while my hometown of Buffalo was number 40! If you want some good old-fashioned New York City crime you'll have to plunk on the couch and watch plotlines concocted by the writers of *Law & Order*, *Castle*, or *Blue Bloods* for actors with phony New Yawk accents.

The only thing I miss about the good old bad days is that if at the last minute you decided to bring someone back to the apartment and it was messy you could always shout, "Oh my God! I've been robbed!"

Chapter 10

CARPE NOCTEM

According to the first city directory, in 1786 every block had a tavern. From a total of 3,340 buildings, 330 sold liquor. The fact that the local water was undrinkable for the first 200 years probably helped contribute to alcohol consumption. Residents often quaffed beer for breakfast, and even children were given alcohol to drink. The completion of the Croton Aqueduct in 1890 and its delivery of fresh water from upstate New York at least helped get rid of the accidental alcoholics.

The intent of Prohibition (1919–1933) was honorable. Alcoholism was rampant, and this took a heavy toll on families. Paychecks habitually went to the barman and never made it home. Children went without food and were forced from school into the workplace.

Despite temperance soldiers and police officers, however, there'd be no end to libations in New York City. German immigrants had brought along their beer-brewing skills, Italians were expert at winemaking, and the Irish brought a talent for consumption. Meantime, a large number of prescriptions contained alcohol and doctors were suddenly writing a lot more of them. Likewise, the use of sacramental wine in churches rose by more than 1,000 percent.

The commercial booze biz went underground, and Manhattan became filled with speakeasies such as Chumley's in Greenwich Village, the Stork Club in Midtown, and the Cotton Club in Harlem. Or as cartoonist Frank McKinney "Kin" Hubbard observed, "Prohibition is better than no liquor at all." My grandfather was working as a waiter in a restaurant where a prodigious amount of "cooking sherry" was kept in the kitchen for regular customers (and staff). Patrons joked about John Winthrop's famous entreaty to build a pure "City upon a Hill" in the New World by calling Manhattan the "City upon a Still."

Prohibition unleashed rampant criminal activity, including a nationwide network of bootleggers and a spectacular rise in gangland violence. With the Depression bearing down hard, president and renowned martini-mixer Franklin Roosevelt decided everyone was in need of a picker-upper, and the government could use the tax revenues, so he repealed the ethanol embargo in 1933. Suffragettes were also indirectly responsible for its demise. Apparently, once the women all got the vote, the men all needed a drink.

By the time I reached New York City there was no shortage of bars and nightclubs to frequent, including the Palladium, Limelight, Area, Heartbreak, Danceteria, and the Roxy. Trendy, pricey, and exclusive Nell's and Stringfellows would open in 1986. Young professionals were hauling in enough money or else had access to large enough expense accounts to support nightly club hopping and champagne popping. Models, celebrities, athletes, artists, rock idols, gossip columnists, self-styled freaks, minor European royalty, and trust fund babies ("celebutantes") melded nicely into the party mix. World-renowned Studio 54 was home to the first glitter bombing during a New Year's Eve bash where four tons of tin foil dropped from the ceiling that people would find in their hair and clothing for months. Eventually, there were allegations of cocaine use and tax evasion at the club – I'm shocked! Throughout the 1980s there existed an alternate after-dark universe particularly attractive to Type A personalities that largely entailed waiting behind a velvet rope outside the city's hottest clubs attempting to look chic enough to be chosen for admittance like a bunch of eager children trying to get picked first for a game of dodgeball. Such velvet-rope profiling led to payoffs, fights, and a great deal of status angst.

"Club kids" partied all night and slept all day. However, I worked in a trading pit on the floor of the stock exchange where it was eardrum-bursting loud and people jumped up and down all day, shouted at each other, mixed vodka into their iced tea, and abused drugs. I didn't see the point of going out at night to a place that was eardrum-bursting loud with people jumping up and down, shouting at each other, and abusing alcohol and drugs. Furthermore, it was already clear from working on Wall Street that alcohol and drugs have a tendency to amplify the disposition, which can be problematic if you're already a jerk to begin with.

Also, I had schoolwork from my night classes at NYU. Most traders popped home after trading ended for their disco naps before joining the aspiring fashion stars, media moguls, technology tycoons, and marketing mavens for a night on the town, an after-party, and a six a.m. breakfast at the Tick Tock diner or the greasy spoon–goodness of Odessa with its kielbasa and eggs. Then it was home to bed or, if it was a weekday, they stumbled straight to work. Early morning flights missed due to late nights on the town were known as Irish Layovers. These were different from Irish Handcuffs, which meant you had a drink in each hand and therefore couldn't carry anything else or open a door.

Manhattan in particular is conducive to a colossal nightlife because with almost the entire island laid out on a grid, it's difficult to get lost and has twenty-four-hour public transportation plus taxis, so there's no place easier for an intoxicated person to safely get home. The club scene continues to roar today with designer drinks and happening DJs and an ever-rotating cast of what's hot and what's not. Some places are strongly promoted while others are supposedly secret and haven't so much as a sign on the door. Recently there was a faux speakeasy in a water tower atop an abandoned Chelsea building where guests had to climb twelve flights of steps and a ladder before emerging through a trapdoor. That will build up your thirst. A number of the hippest spots have moved from the Meatpacking District (which landed the expression "meat market" squarely in double-entendre territory) to Brooklyn – Williamsburg garages, Bushwick warehouses, Gowanus factories, and Red Hook bars. Meantime, I have a secret list of the ten quietest restaurants in New York that I won't be posting online anytime soon.

As for the city's wide variety of music, from Tin Pan Alley ragtime to Harlem jazz-blues and New Wave to No Wave, it endlesly cross-pollinates and transmutes. Composer and bandleader Duke

Ellington noted that musicians were beginning to play a new type of music in the 1910s in the West Indies, New Orleans, and Chicago, but it wasn't until they all converged and coalesced in New York that jazz emerged as a recognized art form in the early 1920s. Forty years later folk music turned to pop music in the Village, and twenty years after that funk became rap in the outer boroughs, the same way that clubs and neighborhoods change along with the tastes and lifestyles of their inhabitants. Greenhorns, dreamers, and carpetbaggers have always been welcome. No proof of residency is required.

The music scene is so diverse that New York must have ten times as many anthems as anyplace else. Take your pick among "The Sidewalks of New York," "Give My Regards to Broadway," "Manhattan," "Take the 'A' Train," "On Broadway," "Spanish Harlem," "Positively 4th Street," "Across 110th Street," "Walk on the Wild Side," "Theme from *New York, New York*," "Fairytale of New York," "No Sleep Till Brooklyn," "New York City," "The Rising," "New York, I Love You But You're Bringing Me Down," and "Empire State of Mind." Or go ahead and create your own siren song, hymn of praise, or litany of complaints for the ultimate New York Mix Tape.

Chapter 11

THE REAL MARCH MADNESS

New York is living proof that the immigrant work ethic leaves the Protestant work ethic in the dust.

It's been said that immigration is the most sincere form of flattery. Nowadays, more than 800 languages are spoken in New York City. In 1855, more than half of all New Yorkers had been born in another country, and by the late 1990s more than a third of all New Yorkers had been born abroad. There are more Irish in New York than in Dublin, more Italians than in Rome, more Jews than in Tel Aviv, more Mexicans than in Oaxaca, more Jamaicans than in Montego Bay, more Puerto Ricans than in San Juan, more Native Americans than in any other city, and more Greek diners than anywhere in the entire world. When I retire I may just go and open an American restaurant in Athens.

The term *melting pot* was originally coined to describe densely populated immigrant neighborhoods on the Lower East Side. So many famous people have emerged from the hubbub and hullaballoo of the Lower East Side that it would take an entire page just to name the musicians. Families may not have been able to afford a private bathroom, but everyone seemed to have an upright piano on the installment plan.

With an almost constant cacophony roaring through their streets, New Yorkers demonstrate that they are listening by interrupting. It's a compliment. They are trying to be helpful when they give names of psychiatrists, allergists, aromatherapists, plastic surgeons, aestheticians, epilators, stylists, personal shoppers, and trainers. Same with when they steadily contradict anyone else attempting to do likewise.

During my first few years in New York I wondered if there were billboards in other countries advertising specific opportunities here. More than 90 percent of shoeshine men in New York City are from Brazil. Are Brazilians genetically gifted shoe polishers the way Kenyans are marathon runners? Is there a rumor in Guadalajara that New York subway riders adore roving mariachi bands and will tip them with gleeful abandon? Did word of a dim sum shortage here reach mainland China? Do Koreans dream of running corner stores and nail salons? Does Nigeria have billboards saying come to Manhattan and sell sunglasses and umbrellas on a New York City street corner? On an overcast day you can get sunglasses for $5 per pair. As the sun emerges from behind the clouds they go up to $7 or $10. Suddenly it starts to drizzle and the table is flipped to display umbrellas. They're $5, but as the rain comes down harder they go to $10 and $15. Talk about entrepreneurship.

An umbrella purchased on the street can sometimes last up to a month, whereas you're lucky if a $25 "Rolex" watch makes it through the end of the week. I recommend the clear plastic umbrellas since you can see when you're about to get hit with another umbrella and do the New York City rainy-day street ballet of raising and lowering yours while others do the same to avoid eye-piercing collisions. The clear umbrella also makes it easier to spot a collapsing crane (the heavy machinery, not the bird).

New Yorkers on the whole are an entrepreneurial lot. During the last transit strike, people were offering to rent themselves out by the hour to help travelers and commuters meet the four-person minimum to drive a car. On TaskRabbit New York City you can find someone to come over and perform just about any job from cleaning, shopping, and cooking to filing, assembling, and research. So much for stranger danger.

The average New Yorker is not racist. This is a city where whites are now in the minority. The current denizens are such a hodgepodge of different cultural backgrounds, where would you start to discriminate and who has that kind of time? Likewise, if there are any homophobes, they're in the closet. Even the selection of mayors has been religiously, racially, ethnically, economically, sexually, and height diverse over the years. Strong female candidates have started running, and certainly we'll have our first woman mayor before long. Bill de Blasio, the current officeholder, appears to have resurfaced from a 1980s Benetton ad with his African American–former lesbian wife and two biracial children. De Blasio is of German and Italian heritage, comes from a broken home, speaks Spanish fluently, admits to liking the Red Sox, is spiritual but not religious, and has tantalized a certain population with the possibility of legalizing ferret ownership. His father was an alcoholic and committed suicide while suffering from inoperable lung cancer. I think that about covers it. Oh, yeah – they live in Brooklyn, of course.

It should be obvious that the skill set for running a maniacal place like New York City, which requires more of a macher than a mensch, is entirely different from that needed to manage the rest of the country. So it doesn't come as a surprise that no mayor has ever gone on to become U.S. president or even vice president. Rudy Giuliani was the most recent to give the national stage a try and between his sketchy associates and messy personal life the public said, "Too New York." But keep your eye on shape-shifting Mike Bloomberg the billionaire. First he was a Democrat, then a Republican, and now an Independent. Maybe one Christmas Day Chinese food will be delivered to the White House.

There aren't many ethnic voting blocs anymore. Spanish Harlem isn't particularly Spanish speaking, while Little Italy has become a pasta and cannoli theme park. Chinatown, that city within a city, is still home to the upside-down dead duck, pig intestines, and shredded jellyfish, but the once-dominant southern Chinese dialect of Cantonese has been eclipsed by Mandarin, the language of most recent immigrants. Most telling of all, wearing a Red Sox cap in New York a decade ago could be fatal, whereas now you might get away with some gentle ribbing or, at worst, a few peanuts to the back of the head.

Basically, the day you arrive here you're a New Yorker. The only downside of a melting pot on such a grand scale is that *everyone* gets a parade, thereby tying up Fifth Avenue from March until November. Most of the year, traffic operates entirely around the schedules of parades, marathons, union demonstrations, and the United Nations. If someone shows up at the office on Monday morning with his or her leg in a cast, it's more likely the result of falling over a police barricade or being mowed down by a grand marshal than a cycling accident. Whereas for the rest of New York State the sugar maple is the official tree and the rose the official flower, the city's tree is the wooden police sawhorse and its flower is the bright orange cone.

As a child growing up in Buffalo I was parade deprived. Sure, there was a spirited St. Paddy's Day march and a Pulaski Day Parade that President Kennedy famously attended in 1962, but we didn't join these. Despite my father being born in New York City in 1931, the year of the movie musical *Manhattan Parade* (which featured the hit song "I Love a Parade"), his parents were both from Copenhagen.

However, when I moved to Manhattan in 1983, the parades began coming to me. Leaving my West Village apartment one Sunday I became an unsuspecting marcher in the Gay Pride Parade amidst queer power chants, rainbow flags, and vinyl bustiers. Likewise, the Halloween pageant in the Village, which extended to salacious theatrical performances on fire escapes, front stoops, and church steps, was something to behold. I'd clearly saved myself a trip to Times Square, though whether for a Broadway show or a burlesque was hard to tell. The months that my friends and I had excitedly invested in creating our Halloween costumes during elementary school were nothing compared with the preparation that went into this extravaganza. If you're going as existentialist Jean-Paul "Hell is other people" Sartre then perhaps the Halloween Dog Parade and costume contest in Tompkins Square Park is more your style. Not surprisingly, the dachshunds and Chihuahuas tend to steal the show since they can really rock a hot dog or bumblebee outfit, but Barknado the shark-attired French bulldog was truly inspired.

The week before the Macy's Thanksgiving Day Parade always reminds me of a kid trying to make friends with someone who has a swimming pool – right before the start of summer. New Yorkers, especially ones with children, desperately attempt to locate a coworker with an apartment near the American Museum of Natural History to watch the floats being inflated on West 77th Street the night before. If the march is on a blustery day, there's the added excitement of a potential mishap – would Sponge Bob escape his shackles and take to the skies? Would Kermit the Frog attack?

Walking home from Wall Street one mild January night I was suddenly in the middle of the Asian Lunar New Year, a profusion of parading dragons, crashing cymbals, leaping acrobats, and exploding firecrackers in the same spot where I normally saw an unsavory selection of seafood and counterfeit Prada bags.

By the middle of March, the Manhattan weather is at its most desolate, but that doesn't bother the hardy St. Patrick's Day paraders. Celts apparently thrive on dreariness, and that's why they compose their music using as many minor chords as possible. Nor are they distracted by therapy appointments. "This is one race of people for whom psychoanalysis is of no use whatsoever," Sigmund Freud is reputed to have said. This is arguably the largest parade in the United States, with exact numbers dependent on whether being in a bar somewhere in the vicinity of the parade route counts as attendance. The first St. Patrick's Day Parade did not take place in Ireland but in Manhattan, when Irish soldiers serving in the English military marched to honor St. Patrick on March 17, 1762, the anniversary of his death. The Irish of Ireland have since co-opted our holiday along with our Lucky Charms cereal. Still, this is the parade that appeals to everyone – the actual Irish, the legacy Irish, the never-been Irish, and the wanna-be Irish, with all becoming true-green for a single day.

Marriage eventually forced a diplomatic move uptown and thrust me into the movie musical, *Easter Parade*. This unofficial event, started right after the Civil War, is a true democracy in that anyone can step out and display their finery, no permit necessary. It's a good place to see live birds' nests in bonnets of real flowers and living proof that polka-dotted mother-daughter dresses will never disappear completely.

A week later comes the Tartan Day Parade, with pipers letting fly with the only two songs taught in bagpipe school – "Scotland the Brave" and "Amazing Grace" – while Scottish terriers line the sidewalks along with some kilt-clad schnauzers trying to pass.

At my job on Wall Street, I had a bird's-eye view of the ticker-tape parade held when the Mets won the World Series in 1986. It was before computers had taken hold, and an overexcited clerk could still toss enough records out the window to put a firm out of business.

On the Fourth of July, which most towns across the United States reserve for their big spectacles, Manhattan, of course, has to be different by celebrating American Independence with a parade in Chinatown. With more than 150 different nationalities in the city, it's as good a place as any. That's the reason most of us came here in the first place – to get away from prying eyes or to find a better opportunity and be, well, independent. We're so independent that we host independence parades for other countries such as Greece, India, the Philippines, Pakistan, and Colombia. In thirty years of going from point A to point B, I've run into the Cuban Day Parade, Feast of San Gennaro Grand Procession, German-American Steuben Parade, Haitian Day Parade, Puerto Rican Day Parade, Captive Nations Parade, African American Day Parade, Three Kings Day Parade, not one but two dog parades, and the Veggie Pride Parade, where people march as giant carrots and pea pods and want to know, "Did your dinner lead a horrible life?"

When a parade passes by, the streets become a riotous arcade of cheering and trumpeting with high steppers and baton twirlers preceding floats that resemble giant wedding cakes. Many families venture out to join the fun and stand side by side with that great American patriot, the street entrepreneur, busily hawking his flags, T-shirts, and sausage-on-a-stick.

Local stores either board up their windows entirely as if a Category 5 hurricane is coming, or else throw open their doors and double up on inventory, and sometimes soda prices, too. Customarily genial doormen become Homeland Security adjuncts, guarding their entranceways to make sure that residential buildings aren't mistaken for national parks. Trapped Fifth Avenue residents groan, "If your country is so fantastic why not go back there?" Call it a Kvetch-22.

With most churches beginning their services at the same time as the parade kickoffs, there's the inevitable collision of worshippers and revelers. This creates such challenges as trying to sing "Be Still, My

Soul" over tubas, trombones, flügelhorns, and double bell euphoniums blasting "Alte Kameraden" and "Frei Weg" during the battle of the oompah-pah bands.

By the time the Carlyle and the Pierre stop serving brunch, the parades are winding down as well. The avenues are filled with police officers directing traffic and street sweepers revving their engines like NASCAR drivers, while marchers yank off plumed hats and pack up their pom-poms, and paradegoers-in-training have their diapers changed. Once again it's possible to walk to Petco near the subway station at 86th and Lexington or Rollerblade to Central Park.

Like most of my peeps in Carnegie Hill, my Upper East Side hood, I've incorporated parades into the tapestry of my life. I don't keep a schedule and thus am regularly surprised to wander out for a calzone and land in a sea of salsa dancers or come face-to-face with a baton-twirling marcher in the Salute to Israel Day Parade. It's inevitable that in a city with more than two dozen big parades a year, some denizens begin to experience parade rage. It can indeed be frustrating to encounter the Irish 165th Infantry when trying to get to the airport, and a few of the parades have a reputation for being overly rowdy. (No names, but one group has the Puerto Rican spindalis as its official bird.)

Overall, it's a joy to witness such festivities. There are so many places in Europe, Asia, and Africa where different tribes, religious sects, and ethnic groups can't seem to get along, but in the New York City primordial soup they live together in the same neighborhoods, and even apartment buildings, without clashing in any significant way. Despite commercials for mood modifiers and a pharmacy on almost every corner, marchers and spectators alike appear to be happy and enjoying a sense of community.

As a kid I used to ask my Danish dad, "When is our parade?" He replied, "It's just us. Whenever we go out it's a parade." So one Sunday every summer I bring a bunch of Danish flags and flag stickers to my Unitarian church, along with some Danish butter cookies, and ask people if they'd like to be in the Danish parade. "What do we do?" (Unitarians love protocol almost as much as they do surveys and Robert's

Rules of Order.) "Just walk home or wherever you're going." Everyone puts on a sticker, takes a flag and a handful of cookies. Because in busy New York City, life is a richer pageant if you love a parade.

Chapter 12

IN THE HOODS

New York is a series of neighborhoods, almost like villages, all with their own dry cleaners, diners, newspaper stands, nail salons, beauty parlors, barbers, grocery stores, movie theaters, pet stores, bars, and local characters. However, you won't see many gas stations or car washes. Nor is the city big on skywalks and subterranean passageways, though it seems they'd make a lot of sense. In Toronto it's possible to go from one end of the city to the other without stepping outside, and these pedestrian warrens are filled with shopping, hair salons, and restaurants. Is someone looking into this? After all, it was the Canadians who brought us the garbage bag, ginger ale, and processed cheese.

Nowadays every corner has a studio for spinning, Pilates, or yoga. Look above the streets and through tall plate glass windows you can see people cycling, stretching, rowing, and running on treadmills. I'm sure upbeat music is being piped in, but I always thought it might be more effective to have someone shouting insults: "Expect to find a partner with that waistline?" and "The transit authority is going to require you to put turn signals on those hips!" New Yorkers are accustomed to responding to anger. The city is without a doubt the capital of the Women's Correctional Facility, with the most beauty parlors, day spas, waxing parlors, electrolysis shops, plastic surgeons, collagen centers, fitness gurus, aromatherapists, and cosmetic dentists per block. In fact, since finding out "laser vaginal rejuvenation" is a real thing, I wouldn't be at all surprised to learn that New York women pay to have their X-rays touched up.

Shopping is the official sport in New York City. Not that proof is necessary, but the shoe floor at tony Saks on Fifth Avenue has its very own zip code – 10222-SHOE. Instead of the vertical tricolor of blue, white, and orange with the municipal seal in the middle, the official New York City flag should be a triangle banner with "Grand Opening" on one side and "Going Out of Business" on the other.

Most neighborhoods have daycare operations (both people and pet) and parks where children can play while their parents or nannies text on their phones. However, there are a few places where no one has seen a child in years – Wall Street and parts of the Garment District, for example. If you bring a small human here, people are liable to stand around staring, trying to guess its age – somewhere between two and twelve.

With the arrival of MetroCards, gone are the token suckers. As a result of quality-of-life campaigns (or crackdowns, such as they are), the squeegee men are mostly gone too. Likewise, no longer does one find guys selling stolen newspapers at a discount on street corners, subway stairwells, and among the backed-up traffic near bridges and tunnels.

All that's really left are the Can People, or "Canners." New York State law requires a deposit on all soda or beer containers, thereby making every discard worth 5 cents to its finder. Redemption is an egalitarian endeavor that attracts as many women as men despite the work being difficult and dangerous. The compact with the Canners is as follows: When exchanging cans for money, they're not allowed to cause lines or disruptions at the supermarkets and in return the management won't bother them. In their quest for cans they're allowed to unpack every bit of garbage on every street so long as they put it all back the way it was. If these protocols are observed, then store clerks, superintendents, residents, and sanitation workers won't harass them. The Canners have territorial battles, but if they're sorted out privately and without violence the police won't give them trouble either. The benefit to the beverage-consuming public is that our streets, parks, and beaches remain clean, and we don't have to feel guilty about throwing away our cans since we know they'll all be redeemed.

New York has a similar system for getting rid of large objects such as rugs and bureaus. There aren't any attics, basements, garages, or town dumps here. Flea markets and street fairs charge a fortune if you want to rent a booth, while inviting the entire neighborhood in for a tag sale isn't advisable. So what to do with an old floor lamp, armchair, table, toaster oven, TV, or computer? Down to the street it goes with a sign saying "Free" and listing the condition, particularly if it's an appliance. Discarded items can last on the curb anywhere from two to ten minutes. Once I was getting rid of six dining room chairs and by the time I came downstairs with the fourth, a guy loading them into a truck yelled, "Hey, lady, over here!" Some people like to observe from a discreet distance as fights between strangers ensue over this stuff. It's good street theater.

A number of neighborhood names are self-explanatory, like Midtown and the Upper East Side. Others must be deciphered. Alphabet City on the Lower East Side has avenues named with a single letter, SoHo is South of Houston Street, NoHo is North of Houston, SoHa is South Harlem, NoMad is North of Madison Square Park, and TriBeCa means Triangle below Canal Street, even though the area is no longer shaped like a triangle. DUMBO is Down Under Manhattan Bridge Overpass. SoBro is the South Bronx. SpaHa means Spanish Harlem, aka El Barrio. Trendsetters are trying to rebrand the Financial District as FiDi, the border between Prospect Heights and Crown Heights as ProCro, and the area right after the Manhattan Bridge Overpass as RAMBO. Meantime, residents of Manhattan's West Side like to refer to it as the Best Side.

Other names can be more confusing. Times Square is not a square and *The New York Times* is no longer there. Turtle Bay has no turtles and no bay. Likewise, Murray Hill has no Murray and no Hill. Coney Island is a peninsula. Duffy Square is more of a trapezoid. Irving Place is named after Washington Irving even though he never lived there. As for the West Side neighborhood that's supposed to be called Clinton or Midtown West, folks persist in calling it Hell's Kitchen the same way some Indians will always refer to Mumbai as Bombay, and everyone ignores the fact that Sixth Avenue was changed to Avenue of the Americas way back in 1945. Most New Yorkers don't even know that the West Side Highway's official designation is the Joe DiMaggio Highway. And Zombieland is the unofficial name for the area around 125th Street and Lexington Avenue where drug addicts are notorious for being unpredictable street crossers.

Some names didn't catch on at all, such as NoBat (North of Battery Tunnel), SoSo (South of SoHo), NoCal (North of Canal Street), and HoBo (where Houston Street intersects the Bowery). UhOh is any neighborhood where if you run out of milk you can't find a store or bodega without traveling more than ten blocks. As for street names, after Force Tube Avenue in East New York, Brooklyn, and Fteley Avenue in Soundview, the Bronx, my favorite is Old New Utrecht Road in Borough Park, Brooklyn.

Long Island is an actual island. So if you're moving about between Manhattan Island and Staten Island and Long Island for Thanksgiving or Hanukkah it's geographically correct to post on Facebook that you're spending the holidays island hopping.

Things aren't much more straightforward when it comes to waterways. The North River is the southern part of the Hudson River, and the East River isn't a river at all but a tidal strait. If you decide to go swimming you'll notice the Hudson has fresh water and the East River is salt. As for drinking water, New York water is not only safe to drink, but tastes terrific and it's free. If you can't afford foam Statute of Liberty crowns, give your friends back home a bottle of New York City water.

I've heard it said that you determine where to live in Manhattan not based on income but on age. Your number of years equals your appropriate street, in other words, nineteen-year-olds should live on 19th Street and eighty-one-year-olds should live on 81st Street. The truth is that it's so hard to find an apartment a person can't look only in one or two neighborhoods. You have to move based on what's available and what you can afford. Live here long enough and you'll know more than one couple staying together because neither partner is willing to vacate the apartment. Divorce isn't just about money and custody of the dog but also rent control, leases, and who gets to hang out at the neighborhood Starbucks. In fact, sharing a rent-controlled apartment has been found to be much more effective in keeping couples together than any prenuptial agreements or marriage counseling. On the other hand, the prospect of giving up a rent-controlled studio apartment has kept many New Yorkers from ever marrying in the first place.

Most city residents live in small, cramped apartments. My father, like many New York infants before and since, had a bureau drawer in his parents' bedroom for a bassinet. Every available square inch counts, and that's why spring cleaning often means taking the short-sleeved shirts and sandals out of the oven and replacing them with the scarves and boots. It's challenging to become a hoarder in a New York dwelling, though some have managed spectacularly, like the two Collyer brothers of Harlem, with more than 130 tons of accumulated possessions.

The city is also one of the few places where it's not uncommon to live with roommates well into your forties. Solitude is rare and considered a luxury, and that's why New Yorkers brag that they've lived in an apartment for ten years and never spoken to their neighbors. For the same reason, there aren't any survivalists in New York. With two roommates and a stationary bicycle in the kitchen, there's no place for beans, gallons of water, a backup generator, and Parcheesi. So bring on the apocalypse, but preferably the day *before* the rent is due.

As a result of the housing situation, New Yorkers tend not to be big on camping. Number one, your first bare-bones living space is basically a campsite. Number two, when you can finally afford $2,000 a month for a studio apartment, heading out into the woods where there are no bathrooms, climate control, or restaurants that will deliver is no different than being homeless. That's why there are no authorized campgrounds in New York City. Whenever we find "nature" inside our apartments we usually try to kill it. Calling a friend over for a late-night extermination has become a predictable scene in any New York–based movie or TV comedy. In fact, one could argue that it doesn't make sense to go on any type of vacation or really even to a park for that matter because of all the rent money you're losing whenever your room sits empty. If a New Yorker is going to die from exposure it'd better be the kind on Gawker or TMZ.

High-density living also makes the appearance of film crews, celebrities, and visiting dignitaries annoying rather than exciting. New Yorkers are not pretending to be cool when they appear irritated by an episode of *Law & Order* shooting out front and the stars lingering on their front stoop. Celebrities can actually have a hard time getting past co-op boards *because* they're famous and it's automatically assumed they have too much *National Enquirer*–style nonsense in their lives for a building where respectable people want to live quietly. The Czech playwright and politician Václav Havel stayed in my building while he taught at Columbia University. He reeked of smoke and his burly entourage was always puffing unfiltered cigs in the driveway next to shiny black SUVs. We weren't entirely surprised to hear that he'd died of lung cancer.

Crammed into apartments together, people must often go out on the street with their cell phones to get some privacy. Don't be startled to see someone arguing, breaking up, and crying on a street corner by phone or in person. However, if there's a hat on the ground it could be performance art. Most people will leave you to your grief, but rest assured that those who do stop to offer comfort will share a much worse problem, along with the numbers of their therapists.

Therefore, it's good to know that New Yorkers don't care if you eavesdrop. They're convinced that their problems are much more interesting than anything going on in your life.

A New York apartment is filled with noises and smells, and not necessarily your own. So many buildings have been reconfigured over the years that someone else's kitchen vent probably leads to your bedroom radiator, hence the unavoidable aromas of soy sausage frying, sauerkraut fermenting, and five-spice cooking. Since lots of New Yorkers are aspiring musicians, you can count on having a house band conducting jam sessions at all hours and telling yourself that you're getting in on the ground floor of the next Mambo Kings. In Buffalo, noises were explained away as the house "settling" or else ghostly inhabitation. In

New York, the noise is strictly the result of boisterous neighbors who are very much alive. There are the de rigueur sounds of passionate lovemaking, crying babies, squabbling teenagers, loud TVs, and barking dogs. With regard to the connections between lovemaking and crying babies, one assumes there's a reminder in there somewhere. As for all the heated debates about whose turn it is to buy toilet paper, it's been said that the only one who listens to both sides of an argument is the person in an adjacent apartment or at the next restaurant table. It just may be that New Yorkers need their noise. They are the second largest users (after people in Hong Kong) of a website called *Coffitivity*, which simulates the sound of a busy coffee shop.

When I arrived in New York there were still a number of buildings with elevator operators – usually an old guy in a uniform that hadn't been cleaned in a few decades with a little wooden stool that had underneath it a transistor radio quietly tuned to a ballgame and a sandwich wrapped in wax paper. Elevator operators in residential and office buildings were often African American. However, in 1984 there were about as many black doormen as black men in that year's Winter Olympics. While the elevator operators have since been rendered obsolete, the diversity among doormen has increased, though there are still about as many women doormen as women in the Oval Office.

Maybe people don't want women doorpeople for fear that they'd be too observant and gossipy: "I can't believe she's wearing those shoes with that suit." "Has he ever heard of a barber?" "I doubt that's going to be a business meeting." "Isn't that yesterday's shirt and tie? Someone had a sleepover." "He wouldn't need to be out with a trainer at six a.m. if he quit the eleven p.m. pizza deliveries." After sorting the prescriptions you might hear: "Look who got Viagra." "She's trying to get pregnant at this age!" "Guess who has an itch?" Women manning the doors might also complain about the temperature. The lobby is cold in the winter, and in the summer the air-conditioning is cranked up to freezing because the doors are constantly opening and letting in the hot outside air. They'd stop and make a huge fuss over babies, too. Then there's the conundrum of whether etiquette-conscious male tenants would have to hold the door for women doorpeople. On the bright side, behind the desk would be static guard, nail glue, and hair spray, and the women would be happy to give restaurant recommendations (and condemnations).

When I was twenty-eight, I had an eighty-two-year-old doorman I wouldn't describe as robust. I found myself regularly dashing to open the door before he could get there and constantly afraid that he'd try and carry packages – mine or anyone else's. For a person raised on the "respect and assist your elders" scheme, there is a real manners conundrum when it comes to having a much older person play the role of helper, even if you're paying him to do so.

Based on the low rate of turnover in the job and the union threatening to walk out once a year, it's safe to assume that doormen make decent money. Doormen who retire early probably go on to get jobs in espionage the way police officers go into the security business. They keep many secrets, even more than bartenders and hairdressers, especially about what gets delivered and who visits in the middle of the night. Doormen smile and pretend they saw nothing, heard nothing, and know nothing just like Sergeant Schultz on *Hogan's Heroes*. I've never read a murder mystery that ends up with the doorman having done it. The more residents have to hide, the more tips they give around the holidays. And speaking of holiday tips: For buildings with lackadaisical superintendents, December is also your one-month window to get anything in the apartment painted or repaired.

The Nature Poets have nothing on New York doormen. These guys are prepared to make eight hours of conversation about the weather every day for more than forty years. Doormen also get paid to listen to a lot of bad jokes. Every time one of my doormen says he has a package for me there's a good chance I'm going to say, "Is it a pony?" Unfortunately, he's not allowed to wallop me over the head with the box or lock me inside the revolving door.

Some people prefer a doorman building because grown children and parents can't visit each other unless they're announced. If kids move from the Midwest to New York, even though the parents fly here to visit they still have to be allowed up and can't just wait for another resident to open the downstairs door and sneak inside. Another strategy is to rent a fifth-floor walk-up knowing the folks can't make it much past the third-floor landing. And New York parents who finally got their children out of rent-controlled apartments can now safely guard the door from any boomerang offspring or laundry stops.

But the doorman system cannot save you from houseguest requests. New York is the number-one tourist destination in the United States. As a result, New Yorkers host more visitors than anyone else, and yet we have the least space for them. With hotels starting at $300 a night plus hefty taxes, long-lost friends and distant relatives are constantly in touch. To New Yorkers, Facebook is a houseguest delivery system. People insist they want to see you, and when you say you'll be away that week they say, "That's okay, just leave the keys." And they think they're being generous by saying that you can come visit them in Duluth, Moose Jaw, or Fishkill anytime at all. Fortunately or not, health quarantines are pretty much a thing of the past, and if you tell people a plague has fallen on your apartment they're certain to declare immunity. Saying that people are already there just leads to, "When are they leaving?" or "We'll just sleep on the couch." Likewise construction: "When is it over?"

The way to get rid of unwanted houseguests, or "house pests" as they're known in studio apartments, is to claim you already have vermin, aka bedbugs. It keeps people out but also markedly reduces your own invitations, and thus is a way of slimming down your social life all around if you're in the mood. My neighbor had bedbugs, and so Henry the bedbug-sniffing beagle came to examine my apartment. Henry declared the place bug free, but in the meantime he peed on a couch and an armchair and crapped in my bedroom, so I'm not all that convinced about his training. The fact that I had my female dogs locked up in the bathroom may have had something to do with his wanting to leave his contact information, so I'll give him the benefit of the doubt. Dating is hard in New York, even for beagles, but he's clearly open to a workplace romance.

Chapter 13

NYIT – NEW YORKER IN TRAINING

My dad grew up at a time when the New York City neighborhood public school system routinely turned out accomplished students. And when it didn't, such as with serial killer David Berkowitz (aka Son of Sam), they could still properly punctuate a sentence. As famed New York newspaper columnist Jimmy Breslin wrote, Berkowitz was the only murderer he ever encountered who could wield a semicolon just as well as a revolver.

Like most people in flyover country, I went to a neighborhood public school. As an only child with divorced parents, this gave me phenomenal stability along with the support of lifelong friends, neighbors, teachers, and my friends' parents. It didn't matter that both of my parents worked since there was always a group of kids to hang out with, and somebody would feed me when it came time for lunch or dinner. Long before "neighborhood watches" became official organizations we already had them on every block in the form of prying eyes who knew you and your family and what you were supposed to be doing or not supposed to be doing. They felt fully entitled to yell at someone else's kids.

It may take a village elsewhere, but in this city we outsource, so every morning phalanxes of babysitters, nannies, and au pairs go into action to get children to their various playdates, kindergarten entrance tutorials, and therapy sessions while updating their Facebook profiles on cell phones. Some families have a nanny for each child à la Brad Pitt and Angelina Jolie, in addition to housekeepers, tutors, drivers, and personal assistants. The last decade has also seen the rise of the "manny," especially where energetic boys or ones who aren't getting enough "male influence" are concerned. These older brothers for hire are able to ride scooters long distances, spend hours at batting cages, never tire of laser tag, and have substantial experience building forts, rockets, and Lego robots. The conventional wisdom may be that women are more nurturing and compassionate, but more and more families are standing by their mannies. And not just for spirited children. New York's adults decided they wanted a manny too, and elected Mayor Mike Bloomberg to three consecutive terms (2002–2014) to straighten up not just the city but its citizenry.

When it comes to educating the kids, New York has chucked neighborhood high schools in favor of something called open enrollment admissions. Why? To promote desegregation, both racial and economic. Kids take subways and buses all over the five boroughs, traversing back and forth to school every day. That makes it difficult for parents to attend school functions such as concerts, conferences, and sporting events, especially if there are other kids in the family with simultaneous activities. Forget farm kids taking a bus twenty miles to school or your grandparents walking a mile in each direction, both uphill. There are teenagers in New York who ride two buses and two subways for two hours and that's just one way! If you take out lunch, gym, and study hall, that was the entire length of my school day. Furthermore, these youngsters lug forty-pound backpacks that make it appear as if they're shipping out with the military or heading to JFK Airport and then on to a product development meeting in Palo Alto.

Sure, some kids saw *High School Musical* and want to go to performing arts school or other specialty schools. Many students attend parochial schools, and obviously Manhattanites are big on Montessori. Imagine if you were going in for heart surgery and saw a diploma on the wall saying your surgeon went to Montessori Medical School. I've always wondered what a space station run by Montessori grads all doing whatever they please would look like. If parents really wanted to do their kids a favor they'd send them to technical school. People who grow up in apartments rarely know how to use a wrench since the building superintendent or a maintenance man does even the simplest repairs.

But for the 90 percent in need of a good but general high school education, there's no reason a neighborhood school shouldn't be able to provide it. If the school has a respectable academic reputation it tends to attract a more racially and economically diverse population than one with a bad ranking. And for all the engineers working on the overcrowding of subways during morning rush hour, a big step would be to remove the several hundred thousand kids clogging the morning commute by having them attend school close to home. On top of everything else, they are three-bowls-of-Trix-cereal awake while the rest of us are still dozing. The only bright side I can see to kids commuting is they can get homework help from the many journalists, editors, and professors on public transportation who make corrections for a living. However, it's hard for them to do homework when they can't sit down or even raise their arms to grab a pen. If we're going to stick with the current commuting kid system, the least we can offer them is study cars with guaranteed seats.

New York students don't tell teachers their homework isn't done because it was run over by the subway or eaten by rats but rather because they were "blocked," the assignment was "too derivative," the espresso machine broke, or they've "renounced directed learning." New Yorkers also have fewer after-school activities as a result of their multiple therapy and tutoring appointments.

Moving on to the younger generation, I feel sorry for elementary-school kids growing up in Manhattan when I compare their life with my free-range childhood of playing in the neighborhood, leaving home after breakfast, and returning when we kids could no longer see the baseball, jacks, or jump rope. However, when we became teens we grew bored, and hanging out at the mall or 7-Eleven was our main form of recreation. Sure, there was still skating, sledding, and soccer, but by then those activities were considered kid stuff. City teenagers have it great in that they can walk or take public transportation to stores, arcades, events, movies, and restaurants.

At least they could walk if their parents would let them. I now present you with The Great Stroller Controversy. If tourists see a picture of a stroller with a red slash through it they may not understand the nature of this protest. Children of an age who can and should be walking and have no disabilities are pushed around in strollers because it's more convenient for parents (and provides a place to hang shopping bags along with a Frappuccino holder). Singles and couples who have not procreated, along with those whose offspring have grown and gone, claim this clogs up already narrow pedestrian walkways, staircases, subways, and so forth. The parents are eventually going to teach those kids to walk, right? Were they so busy studying for preschool and kindergarten exams that the whole personal mobility thing got overlooked?

This wasn't really an issue until the 1990s, when fertility treatments suddenly led to an explosion of multiple births in the city. As a result, the innocuous single-wide stroller suddenly became a high-tech double- or even triple-wide deluxe stroller known as a "travel system," complete with swivel seats and foot-activated dual-rear parking brakes. You'll find them blocking sidewalks, doorways, and store aisles, thus causing pedestrian gridlock. They require runways, traffic police, and parking garages.

Meantime, the eight-year-olds riding in these strollers as minivans are rarely disciplined for bad behavior, but told to "make better choices." New York parents feel that doing permanent psychological damage to their children is much more effective than disciplining them. Then again, these children use their experiences to write award-winning angst-filled TV sitcoms, movies, plays, books, video games, and comedy shows, and are able to pay for their parents to retire to Florida as well as hire a good limousine service for themselves.

Having lots of different schools accessible to lots of students can make for intense competition. Most parents are going to spend thousands of hours helping their children with homework. When I was a kid and we asked our parents how to change miles into kilometers or solve for a square root they looked at us as if we'd lost our minds, and said stuff like "Everything is different now" or "We used a slide rule" (a *what*?) or "Never saw anything like that before. Maybe I was absent that week." True, with kids nowadays getting the homework a grad student received in my time, parental involvement is mandatory. Everything those parents forgot or missed during the first eighteen years of life will now be revisited and relearned. In case they thought they'd read the *Aeneid* or did a logarithm for the last time, it's all coming back, only this time on a notebook computer and with gender-neutral examples.

It's often been said that there are two kinds of people in the world – givers and takers, optimists and pessimists, lovers and haters, those who make things complicated and those who make things simple, those who like Neil Diamond and those who don't. "There are two kinds of people in this world," wrote Robert Benchley in his *Law of Distinction*, "those who believe there are two kinds of people in the world and those who don't." City parents are raising one of two kinds of New Yorkers – door holders or door closers. Living in an elevator society, most of us are constantly faced with the choice of whether to throw our arm in front of the doors and let the people following close behind inside, or else scrunch ourselves into the front corner that's out of view while frantically pressing the "door close" button in an otherwise empty car.

Sometimes I'm surprised by who turns out to be a door closer versus a holder, especially when it comes to celebrities and famous politicians, and other times I'm not at all surprised. Then there are the Tony Award–worthy performances by those pretending to be hitting the "door open" button, smiling like a gracious host and wildly gesturing you aboard while pounding on the "door close" button and then looking crestfallen and apologetic when you don't make it. This category will be called Best Fake Nice Person in an Almost Empty Elevator. I'm not saying there's going to be an Elevator Judgment Day at the end of life's ride, but when New Yorkers lay their heads down at night they know in their hearts whether they're holders or closers, and just like being a subway pole leaner on crowded trains, there's still time to change.

Chapter 14

I'VE ALWAYS DEPENDED ON THE KNISHES OF STRANGERS

When my grandfather was first working in Manhattan and experienced periods of unemployment, he'd buy a bunch of bananas for 5 cents, and those would last him two days. When I arrived in the city with a bank account in the low two digits, I found that combining a soft pretzel with a soda created some sort of chemical reaction that filled me up for the entire day. Likewise, a bowl of lentil soup with a roll also did the trick. Other NYU students lived on bagels bigger than hockey pucks, ramen noodles, and Entenmann's pastries. It may not be desirable to eat on less than $5 a day, but it can be done. The main difference between Buffalo and New York City cuisine was that menu items here seldom contained the word *surprise*, crushed potato chips, or cream-of-mushroom soup casserole.

Despite Manhattan's reputation as a racy city, you'll rarely hear women utter four letter words such as *cook, iron, wash, mend, dust,* or *fold.* "What does a real New Yorker make for dinner?" Reservations. And the more impossible the restaurant is to get into, the better it is, just like with doctors, schools, shows, food co-ops, and pole dancing classes. How can it possibly be any good if you can get a reservation, appointment, interview, ticket, or place within six months' time without knowing someone?

Most New Yorkers have more takeout menus than cookbooks. They jam every drawer, are used to scribble notes, plug leaks, do origami, housebreak puppies, line birdcages, roll joints, and stabilize tables and bedsteads. Takeout is to the New Yorker what the buffalo was to the Native Americans – giver of all life. As a result, New Yorkers will pay just about any price for home delivery. Along with breakfast, lunch, and dinner, it's routine to order some batteries for the TV remote in the morning, a can of cat food in the afternoon, and a tube of toothpaste before bed. To get to the store, you'd have to go all the way down in the elevator and then walk to the corner.

Food delivery is not just for offices and apartments. People regularly have entire meals delivered to their cars while waiting for alternate-side-of-the-street parking to kick in or while picnicking in the park. Kids order breakfast and lunch delivered to their schools (sometimes through a restroom window). Cops order deliveries on the streets they're patrolling. Boats pull up to piers to meet the guy with their BBQ spare ribs and sodas. Bands order food delivered to the weddings they're playing. And the truly brazen order meals to be delivered to restaurants if they're part of a group but don't like what's on the menu. Still, I think the prize goes to the guy who had a pizza delivered during a Shakespeare in the Park production of *The Trojan Women*, a tragedy about people starving in a prisoner-of-war camp. Evidently he didn't learn in kindergarten that you're supposed to bring enough for everyone.

There are more than 20,000 restaurants in New York, from four-star places with world-famous chefs to checkered tablecloth bistros and hole-in-the-wall joints. Most are affiliated with some ethnicity or another. The only thing I've never seen is a Canadian restaurant, unless you count the dozen or so Tim Hortonses. The four major New York food groups are Chinese, Italian, Mexican, and Indian. Irish coffee contains the other four food groups: caffeine, alcohol, sugar, and fat. Cronuts (a croissant/doughnut hybrid) are New York's equivalent of the state fair's deep-fried Twinkie. Cake balls are the new cronut, and one of the best places to load up on these is at Ronnie's in the Essex Street Market on the Lower East Side. Guinea pig is on the menu at a few restaurants in heavily Ecuadorian sections of the city, though sometimes you must call ahead to order it. And if you wake up hankering for the home-cooked Himalayan food from a past life, try the terrific Top Café Tibet in Ditmas Park, Brooklyn. The dumplings are to die again for.

There are more than a dozen Ray's pizzerias in New York but few family-style restaurants. With space limited and tables jam-packed, it's already loud enough without a fight going on. If a restaurant has a sign saying it's closed for renovations with no reopen date, this means it's been condemned by the health department. Either payoffs weren't made or they weren't accepted. Rent in New York is too high – if your restaurant needs repairs you bring in a crew and do it overnight or during a slow weekend.

After street vendor food, Chinese is the default cuisine in New York because most everyone can find something they like and there's plenty that's free of the dreaded lactose-gluten-nut triumvirate. It's reasonably priced, the restaurants are almost always open, and the meal is at your door by the time you've poured a drink. If you're dieting there's not much temptation as far as dessert goes since they're basically inedible except for the sliced orange and stale fortune cookie. There's a theory that one enormous Chinese kitchen operates underneath the city and shuttles the food to all the different neighborhoods from there. When ordering, it's best to use the numbers alongside the menu. The phone operators and waiters have little knowledge of English and usually sport name tags that say Tom, Bill, and Mike. Because people tend to order the same thing with some degree of regularity, the *Sex and the City* scene where a Chinese restaurant phone operator knows Miranda's order by heart and giggles at her is pathetic but all too familiar.

The Slow Food Movement, which has more than 100,000 members in 45 countries, arose in France and Italy in the 1980s as a backlash against societal and culinary velocity, and decrees that a good meal should take several hours. (France is also where career waiters can't be fired, even for surly service, and earn salaries that don't incorporate tipping, so they needn't worry about turning tables or paying their rent.)

However, the Slow Food Movement has made barely a ripple in this Syncopated City. In fact, the words *Grab and Go* regularly appear in deli and diner windows as a major selling point. Restaurants want to turn their tables several times a night. And while it's true that people in other burgs may eat a breakfast sandwich or a rolled-up slice of pizza on the run, New Yorkers can consume a three-course meal and beverage while racing to catch the F train.

Few eateries were willing to risk having outdoor tables in the 1970s and '80s for fear that the customers would "chew and screw" or if they did pay, the cash would be snatched by a passerby. It wasn't an optimal experience for patrons either, as they were often panhandled, cursed, and solicited while trying to enjoy a burger and bus fumes. Nowadays almost every block has tables outside in nice weather, and customers relax with their friends and dogs and many are able to smoke. Why, it's almost like Gay Paree, just without the churlish wait staff, dog crap everywhere, and anti-gay marriage protesters.

Waiters and waitresses across the country are known for being hyphenates, usually as waiter-actors or waitress-musicians, although I've heard actresses paying the bills with temp work refer to themselves as "temptresses." New York City servers tend to be at least triple hyphens, such as waiter–tour guide–blogger or waitress–visual artist–Olympian-in-training. Like their French comrades, they also have a reputation for impatience, though you can never be sure if they're "in character" for an audition. On more than one occasion I've been brought something completely different from what I ordered, such as a meat dish instead of a vegetarian one, and after pointing out the error was asked, "So does that mean you don't want it?" Still, New York diners themselves have a reputation for being an exacting, complaining lot so I can't say the attitude is completely unexpected. Manhattan servers have been known to ask recalcitrant customers, "Is *anything* okay?"

There is a prepared food store called Lorenzo & Maria's Kitchen on the Upper East Side of Manhattan. Maria screams at her employees, suppliers, and customers all day long. My friends and I regularly e-mail one another the scathing Internet reviews about her shrieking barrages of abuse at anyone and everyone. Two of our favorite reviews are:

"Very odd environment" and "There is often a lot of noisy vocalizing going on – usually management getting angry with customers on the phone." "Management" would be Maria. There are no other authority figures. In fact, the staff tends to silently cower under her malevolent gaze. I don't speak Spanish, but another patron told me that she's particularly insulting and obscene in that language. There are no prices listed on anything. Yet, they've been in business for more than forty years. The food is delicious. Customers make recommendations to others standing in line – you must try the beef Wellington and potatoes Anna – if it's possible to speak above the hollering. I'm in there at least once a week, wearing noise-canceling headphones. I've never seen Lorenzo and am petrified to ask about him, though it's probable his leave-taking involved a massive amount of shouting.

One of the more colorful restaurants in New York is the family-owned and operated Shopsin's, previously located in Greenwich Village for thirty years and now at the Essex Street Market on the Lower East Side. For decades it wasn't listed in any guidebooks (by threat of owner and chef Kenny Shopsin), and so before the Internet you had to know about it to go there. If a potential customer phoned and asked if they'd contacted the restaurant, Kenny replied that it had closed and was now a shoe store. There were rules about how many people could be in your party (no more than five), and you couldn't split your party and pretend to be two separate parties. When the French ambassador was turned away, a nasty letter was sent on diplomatic stationery and promptly framed and displayed in the window. If people asked to look at a menu, Kenny's wife, Eve, who worked as hostess and waitress, said it would be like allowing them to look in her husband's underwear drawer. When I brought an older minister with me for lunch, Eve looked him up and down and announced, "You'll have the diet plate," to his great shock. Sometimes models would stroll in, order food, and not eat it. Eve would put the leftovers off to the side and finish them during her shift. If asked what a certain dish was like she could be counted on to reply, "It's a nice plate of food." If asked about the contents she said, "Whatever Kenny feels like." A famous food critic ordered several different dishes and Eve said, "No, that's a waste of food." He explained that he was a restaurant reviewer and planned to pay for everything. She told him he could have one entrée and either an appetizer or a dessert. When a customer ordered a cheese enchilada appetizer and a cheese tortellini entrée, Kenny refused, saying the man wouldn't be regular for a week, though not in those exact words. The place is always bustling, and it just goes to show you that deep down New Yorkers secretly like to be taken charge of. But you need to earn their submission.

The best movie theater usher I ever saw was a retired school bus driver. He shrieked at people to get in line, to stay in line, to be quiet in line, and threatened them with expulsion. A fifty-year-old woman sheepishly raised her hand and asked permission to use the lavatory. It's such a demanding city that there's actually a certain amount of relief in knowing that someone else is in control, especially someone as highly qualified in keeping miscreants under wraps as a high school bus driver. Let him guard against the line-jumpers, and there are many.

While service in New York varies from restaurant to restaurant, the food on balance is good. There's too much competition to get away with serving unappetizing fare. So it's easy to get meals containing fresh ingredients at reasonable prices. Even farm-to-table restaurants are gaining in popularity. Heavy turnover and foot traffic ensures that nothing sits around too long. New York is known for a number of foods, in particular hot dogs (if not the quality then the prevalence), cheesecake, Italian ice, Waldorf salads, bagels, baked pretzels, and pizza. However, when I moved here the pizza in Buffalo was better than New York's and it's still better. Even Dad had to concede that point.

New York is also famous for eastern European Jewish cuisine, including celery soda, pastrami, brisket, corned beef, lox, cream cheese, potato pancakes, kugel, babka, knishes, dill pickles, matzo ball soup, chopped chicken liver, challah bread, gefilte fish, blintzes, rugelach, and egg creams (milk, soda water, and vanilla or chocolate syrup – *no* eggs or cream). New York actor Zero Mostel, the son of eastern European Jews, declared, "Romanian-Jewish cooking has killed more Jews than Hitler." At Sammy's Roumanian Steakhouse on the Lower East Side they have bottles of schmaltz – pure, bright yellow chicken fat – on the table in case there's not enough fat on your brisket. *Chalushes* (khal-ush-ess), by the way, is Yiddish for "nausea." My thrifty father's favorite Manhattan eatery was Dubrow's Cafeteria in the Garment District, where he regularly enjoyed a bowl of cold borscht. Over the sounds of robust kibitzing and noshing he'd say, "The streets of New York might not be paved with gold, but at Dubrow's seltzer flows from the water fountain."

When I first moved to the city, most New York specialty food wasn't available in the rest of the country, or if it was, it wasn't nearly as good. After my father retired to New Mexico I had to send him a monthly fix of pastrami and rye bread. However, bagels are the best example. The steamed and frozen Lender's "bagels" I was raised on were rubbery and tasteless compared with baked, boiled, and seasoned New York bagels. Back then many of the famous New York bagel shops had delivery services and would express their products overnight around the country. Nowadays it's possible to enter a bakery in almost any town and get a decent bagel with a schmear of anything from a dozen different flavors of cream cheese to peanut butter. The only difference is that New York bagels technically have zero calories since they're usually consumed while running to catch a train.

Chapter 15

TWELVE ANGRY NEW YORKERS

One could make a case that New York is actually a great city for shy people because they can disappear into a crowd and mostly avoid the pleasantries required for one-on-one encounters. This would not be correct. Chutzpah prevails here. *Chutzpah* is a Yiddish word typically described as a guy who kills his parents and then begs for mercy because he's an orphan. A colleague's wife was walking in Times Square when she looked down and saw a man's hand atop her open purse. The explanation: "Oh, I saw it open and was just closing it for you." Chutzpah was perhaps best exemplified by Mayor Ed Koch who said, "I'm not the type to get ulcers. I give them." And after not being reelected in 1989, "The people have spoken, and now they must be punished!"

However, one need not be Jewish to be a contender. Real estate entrepreneur, reality show star, and Queens native Donald "The Donald" Trump is a purveyor of fine chutzpah with statements such as, "Let me tell you, I'm a really smart guy," and "I'm not a schmuck. Even if the world goes to hell in a handbasket, I won't lose a penny." Likewise, Republican senator Alfonse D'Amato when he called his Democratic rival Chuck Schumer "a putzhead" in the 1998 election and proceeded to lose. The Paris, a 581-seat single-screen theater on West 58th Street, is an archetype of chutzpah. It shows one movie all month long – if you don't like it too bad. In New York City the shy person will not get taxis, dates, or restaurant service, and most important, will not be equipped to deal with impudent New Yorkers. As a result, therapists, support groups, and assertiveness trainers are standing by, ready to fix all of the chutzpah-challenged.

In 1964 the city, and to some extent the nation, became transfixed by a story about a twenty-eight-year-old woman named Catherine "Kitty" Genovese who was stabbed to death in Queens, and despite thirty-seven onlookers, no one came to her aid. This developed into an urban myth used to exemplify how New Yorkers were callous, irresponsible, and only out for themselves. However, on closer inspection, the "evidence" for this portrayal of apathetic bystanders turned out to be laden with inaccuracies. The truth is that if you are in distress, people will help you. The exception, then and now, is that there exists in the population a number of illegal immigrants, people with arrest warrants, and parole violators who are compelled to assist anonymously or not at all.

Try not giving a pregnant woman, or an elderly or physically challenged person a seat. First come the glares and the throat clearing. If you still haven't received the message, a confrontation will follow, often laced with sarcasm. "Excuse me" is almost always meant as a threat rather than an apology. Similarly, "Thanks a lot" means a particular behavior should *not* be repeated *or else*. I've watched riders gang up on a bus driver who tried to keep people from boarding when the passengers insisted there was more room. I've seen young parents stopped and told their baby is facing the wrong way in a Baby Bjorn, and on cold days admonished that their youngster should be wearing a hat. Then there was the prosecution of couple who left their child bundled up outside a restaurant on a winter day. The mother is Danish, and the practice is common in Scandinavia. First a waiter said it was too cold outside for the baby and too loud inside for them to be able to hear the baby. Next, a patron called 911 after seeing the unattended child. The parents were arrested (though the charges were eventually dropped) and the child was briefly put into foster care. The mother became an honorary New Yorker when she turned around and sued the police for false arrest (but lost).

New Yorkers will also tolerate a great deal of local color. You can do gymnastics, breathe fire, sing, shout, preach, beg, bang a washtub and they'll keep reading their newspapers. Radioman is the nom de New York of an eccentric homeless man with a boom box around his neck who has appeared in more than 100 films and TV shows. Then there was the guy who went by the name Adam Purple in the East Village and wore purple from head to toe, created gardens in empty lots, and subsisted on money earned from redeeming cans. Self-taught architect Arthur Wood built what is best described as a "Dr. Seuss house" in the Clinton Hill section of Brooklyn.

But New Yorkers do not ignore small injustices. They are strong, dedicated, and theatrical self-policers. It's like the Wild West where we've all been deputized to keep the peace in our own backyards. Just try not picking up after your dog – you will immediately hear the passive-aggressive, "Do you need a Baggie?" or the accusatory "You forgot to clean up after your dog." An order for a sidewalk vendor such as "Can I have a pretzel?" has been known to elicit, "Can I have a *please?*" Finding yourself stuck in traffic and complaining to the cabbie "I should've walked" may very well prompt him to say, "I should've been a lawyer." If you drop money or a scarf, it's true that there's a chance you won't get it back, but try dropping a cigarette butt and there's an excellent chance you will. If there are women around and you spit on the ground you may not get it back, but after they've finished tsking and scowling you'll wish you could.

I've met organ donors who want to be able to designate whether their parts go to Democrats or Republicans. (Independents could give one kidney and one lung to each.) So New Yorkers care. A lot.

That said, this sense of civic responsibility rarely carries over to jury duty. Few New Yorkers want to sit on a jury. And it's a shame because you meet the most fascinating people and hear dialogue better than anything on *Law & Order*. Jury duty should be mandatory for method actors and crime writers. It also falls under the category of patriotic duty. If young people are putting their lives on the line to defend this country, then the rest of us should be able to get to the jury bullpen by nine a.m. The orientation video reminds us that it took the better part of two centuries for blacks and then women to be allowed to serve on juries. But the cost of living in the metropolis is high, the trip to the courthouse inconvenient, going through security a pain, and starry-eyed wannabes didn't move here to decide whether the pothole was really that dangerous or the pedestrian was more likely staring at her phone. Most New Yorkers are trying to create a career, build a business, or get their "name in electric lights" as the hero says to his mother in *The Jazz Singer*.

Unfortunately, there aren't enough idle retirees and people who want to take time off from their salaried positions to fill the demand for jurors, so popular water cooler conversation in New York is about how to escape jury duty. On Wall Street, where missing a single day can mean losing out on the opportunity of a lifetime, employees had it down to a science.

1. *Don't* tell them you can't afford to go, show up dressed like an Austrian archduke, carry a hemorrhoid pillow, or make an incendiary statement such as you hate cops. They've heard all 8 million. You can give all the schedule conflicts in the world but they'll just ask for a date that works. They don't care since they have forever.

2. *Don't* fill out the paperwork in an illegible scrawl the way my coworker did. They'll just offer you an interpreter.

3. *Do* throw away jury summonses for as long as possible. They don't arrive via registered mail so there's no way to prove you received it. Once the correspondence reaches an uncomfortably high threat level the best thing to do is produce a doctor's note saying that you're mentally ill, have to pee a lot, or have a back injury. They attempt to fine the duckers and dodgers, but no one has ever gone to jail. Once you sit in a courtroom you'll realize they have bigger problems to prosecute than errant jurors.

I've heard of only one person who was punished (with community service), and that was because he sent a substitute in his place. Apparently he thought the Civil War was still going on. However, if you have a graduate degree in anything you may just as well go and wait since few people with advanced degrees ever get selected to sit on a Manhattan jury. My father, who was a state supreme court reporter for thirty years, liked to say, "A lawyer's worst nightmare is to have someone on the jury who is capable of thinking."

Although they say there's no age limit, if you're over sixty-four then just write in large, shaky letters, "I'm too damn old," and send it back. But be sure to spell "too" correctly so they'll think you have a graduate degree. Jury clerks have a reputation for being tough, which is why when one woman's husband received a summons, she put a sprinkling of his cremated ashes in a Baggie and sent them on down to the courthouse.

To be fair, jury duty has improved tremendously over the past thirty years. The jury rustlers are now nice to you, a stipend is paid that actually covers your costs for transportation and a modest lunch, and the bullpen is wired for the Internet, well lit, and climate controlled. If you live in a crowded apartment or have houseguests, it's not a bad place to spend the week. I sat next to a guy who finished an entire screenplay (in which zombies take over New York, what else?), while another woman completed her tax returns (which were "messy after the divorce"). They were both pleased to have been forced to finish the tasks by direct order of the Constitution.

Recently, New Yorkers have become excited by a decision in California to include noncitizens who are permanent legal residents in the jury pool. That would be perfect since we have plenty of immigrants, it's an automatic problem solver and truly patriotic – getting others to do the jobs we don't want is the American Way.

Chapter 16

URBAN
DICTIONARY

When I was growing up in Buffalo it was incredibly exciting if a president came to visit. Older folks proudly regaled us with having once met JFK (my uncle Jim), Eisenhower (Dad), or even FDR (Mom). A presidential stopover infused the air with a holiday atmosphere – shops closed, welcome signs were made, people took off from work and school to line the streets hoping for a glimpse of the great man himself. My relatives were not subject to background checks beforehand or tackled by Secret Service during these casual encounters.

New York City is not like that. The five worst words you can hear on the news in the morning are "The president is in town." This means traffic will be backed up for hours. Fail to the chief. Despite the fact that New Yorkers are Democrats by about five to one, they have no desire to see the president, even a Democratic one. The next worst gridlock inducer is when the United Nations convenes. It isn't just a matter of all the delegates and their entourages arriving in the city, but also escorts, rent boys, and dominatrices from up and down the East Coast. If you think it's hard to get a hotel room when the UN is in town, just try getting into a strip club.

That's why they call it The City That Never Sleeps. I once got in a taxi where the driver stopped at a corner and swapped with another driver. It turns out that the two were brothers-in-law, both wore turbans, and they shared a single cab and cab license. The taxi was on the road 24 hours a day, 365 days a year and they changed shifts on street corners. I also had a fruit and vegetable vendor on my block who lived underneath his stand (and was surely taking cash under the table). If you had an apricot emergency or a sudden craving for Vidalia onions, it was possible to go out and buy some from him at four in the morning.

Being a twenty-four-hour city, New York requires several shifts of workers, so at any given time of day or night people are heading to and from work on subways and buses or taking care of errands and visiting the gym while off work. I've heard that in Chinatown beds are rented not by the month or week or even the day, but by the shift – you can hire a pallet to sleep on for eight hours. When I first moved here from a community where everyone aside from hospital workers and snowplow operators worked from eight to four, I couldn't figure out who all these non-homeless people were hanging around diners and parks during regular work hours. It was before cell phones and laptops and the only people who worked from home were envelope sealers and phone sex operators. Most were clearly not stay-at-home parents picking the kids up from school. I finally determined that aside from the tourists, swing-shift zombies, drug dealers, and trust fund recipients, the rest had to be farmers – paid by the government not to grow corn and soybeans or raise cattle.

New York has had various nicknames over the years, some more famous than others: Goats' Town, The Golden Door, Gotham, The Big Apple, the Empire City, A Town So Nice They Named it Twice, City of Critics. New York City is sometimes called the Capital of the World, despite the fact that it's not the capital of the country or even of New York State. However, New York served as the U.S. capital from 1785 to 1790 (which is why George Washington slept and ate basically everywhere), and most New Yorkers are under the impression this is still the case.

Manhattan is an island, but just like Madagascar, Hilton Head, Bermuda, and Alcatraz, you don't say, "I'm going to Manhattan Island." However, the rest of the local islands, including Long, Staten, City, Ellis, Governors, Roosevelt, Shelter, Coney, Fire, Block, and Rikers do require the "Island" designation. You wouldn't tell people you're off to visit friends on Long, Shelter, or Fire. Don't worry if this sounds confusing, since a recent survey showed that 90 percent of New

Yorkers couldn't identify Staten Island on a map. However, any Manhattan schoolchild can tell you that the sun rises on the Upper East Side and sets on the Lower West Side, the North Star floats above Yankee Stadium, and the quickest way to get to Antarctica is from the South Ferry subway station.

People often refer to Manhattan, the smallest of the five boroughs, as "New York" or "New York City" or simply "The City." Technically these terms aren't correct because New York is a state and New York City is composed of four other boroughs, sometimes called the "outer boroughs" – Brooklyn, Queens, Staten Island, and the Bronx. Which brings us to the fact that the Bronx is never just "Bronx," just like you would never say, "I'm taking Thruway." To further complicate matters, Brooklyn and Queens are technically on the whale-shaped Long Island. Meantime, all the boroughs have their own counties. However, Manhattanites are the only people who cannot tell you the name of their county (New York). Or how big an acre is. Or the speed limit. They know blocks. They can give you the size of any distance in city blocks. There is a famous *New Yorker* cover by Saul Steinberg that depicts a map with a westward view from Ninth Avenue in which the world recedes from the city as if it's all insignificant exurbia. Perhaps this explains why when New Yorkers say "The City" no matter where in the world they are, they expect people to know they're talking about Manhattan.

Which brings us to "The Country." When people in New York say they are going to "The Country," they're not talking about the scent of manure drifting in from the west and crop dusters buzzing overhead. From the first day of spring through Labor Day, well-to-do New Yorkers can be overheard in elevators saying they are coming from or on their way to "The Country." What country are they talking about you may well ask – Canada? No, these folks are going to Long Island – Mattituck or Quogue or Hampton Bays – an exit on the Long Island Expressway approximately two hours east with no traffic (which has *never* happened).

When my grandfather moved to Huntington in 1939 the population of 1,401-square-mile Long Island was about 4 million, and the eastern half was indeed almost entirely cranberry bogs, backwoods and farmland. Fast-forward seventy-five years and the population has doubled to practically 8 million people, making it one of the most crowded islands in the world, ahead of Ireland, Singapore, and Sicily. So nowadays you're basically five minutes from a Lululemon, SoulCycle, TCBY, Trader Joe's, and Whole Foods. The streets are fully paved, the mailing addresses don't say Rural Route, and there's plow service in winter. There are no cows, horses, or pigs in their yards. These lots aren't even zoned for turkeys. People don't awake to the arrival of the hay truck, get scraped in the eyeball while milking cows, or find a rattlesnake curled up in the barn. They just can't bring themselves to say the word *suburbs*. The "country folk" who live there year-round refer to these interlopers as "cidiots" (city + idiots). Oddly, it turns out that one of the main reasons for moving to New York is to make enough money to move out of New York.

The aforementioned Long Island Expressway is also known as the World's Longest Parking Lot or the Home of the Thirty-Five Car Pileup, and where thousands have died, including singer Harry Chapin and director Alan J. Pakula. As a child being driven to Huntington to visit my grandfather, I was fascinated by the daredevil skid marks that went straight up the median. In Western New York the only place you could find those was at the Lancaster Speedway, which featured a racing oval in addition to a drag strip.

When I moved to New York City from the Chicken Wing Belt and everyone asked where I was from (the accent was a giveaway, though the locals didn't seem to be aware that they all sounded like Mel Blanc's cartoon characters) and I said New York, I was quickly corrected. It turns out that rubes from Buffalo, Rochester, Syracuse, Utica, and Albany aren't allowed to say "I'm from New York" or "I'm a New Yorker" to five-borough New Yorkers. The term *Upstate New York* had to be invented to keep northerners paying low rent from gaining any prestige. New York is the only state with an official "upstate" to delineate the cool people from the merely cold people. Manhattanites who are part of the downtown club or art scene can be even more discerning – they don't distinguish between upstate and uptown.

Above 14th Street is strictly nosebleed territory to them, and they only go to the Upper East Side to be hospitalized.

New Yorkers who live in the outer boroughs, along with those who visit the city from Long Island, New Jersey, Connecticut, and Westchester, and come to the city to work, shop, or see a show are often called B&T or BNT ("bridge and tunnel") people or BBQs (Brooklyn, Bronx, and Queens). Growing up, I knew only one New York family – the Bunkers, who starred in the politically and socially provocative sitcom *All in the Family* from 1971 to 1979. Archie said "tirlit" instead of "toilet" and called a person who had a sex change operation a "transtesticle."

Chapter 17

I Saw Mommy Kissing the Tree Man

Here is the New York calendar from when I first moved to the city. Fall meant a teachers' strike. December meant a transit strike. Spring meant a baseball strike. Summer meant a garbage strike, usually during a heat wave. Christmas meant that Jews went to a double feature followed by a Chinese restaurant.

No place can do the holiday season like New York. You turn the corner to your apartment, the same corner you round several times a day all year-round and are suddenly hit with the scent of fresh pine along with the sight of two guys in snowsuits relaxing in lawn chairs, looking as if they're inside a living room rather than outside in the cold.

The day the Christmas tree men arrive is officially the first day of the holiday season, like the first time you see the tulips on Park Avenue it's spring and the first time the UPS drivers don their shorts it's the start of summer. The tree men come down from the north, mostly Maine and Canada, and for a month they live on their corner lot, a few sleeping in their vans at night, but most have linked up with locals after visiting the same blocks year after year and believe it or not, are invited to live for free on couches and futons in apartments. For New York women, it's the equivalent of a citywide Victoria's Secret parade. These rugged, gainfully employed frostbacks often make themselves available for hot cocoa and conversation, with more than a few extending their stays into the new year after cozying up to a particularly discerning customer.

Many people also celebrate Kwanzaa, the Winter Solstice, and Hanukkah. Like Rosh Hashanah and Yom Kippur, Hanukkah is always described as early or late. The Jewish holidays, it seems, are never on time. A tree and a menorah are assembled in most lobbies just to make sure that residents enjoying the tippling season don't overlook the tipping season.

At holiday time New York beckons to out-of-towners from the tristate area, across the nation, and around the world with its gaily decorated store windows, Nutcracker performances, manger at St. Patrick's Cathedral, toy selection at FAO Schwarz, and aroma of roasting chestnuts wafting from street carts. Then there's Rockefeller Center, aglow with its skyscraper-high tree, while featuring ice-skaters, shoppers, and the Radio City Christmas show. You haven't lived until you've seen thirty-six racially and ethnically (though not height and weight) diverse women dancing around in red suits and white whiskers pretending to be an imaginary fat man. All the mayhem is finally capped off by a ball dropping in Times Square on New Year's Eve. For therapists as well as local chapters of AA and Weight Watchers, December is known as "the busy season." Stores put up signs saying "Happy Holidays" and in small letters underneath write, "Some restrictions may apply."

As if it's not enough that New Yorker Peter Cooper came up with Jell-O, a few other creative natives gave us modern-day Christmas. Washington Irving Americanized the Dutch Sinterklaas as a potbellied philanthropist in a horse-drawn wagon in his 1809 satirical history of New York. A local bookseller named William Gilley published a poem in 1821 about Santa along with an illustration of a sleigh on a rooftop being pulled by a single reindeer. Two years later, Chelsea author Clement Clarke Moore added seven more reindeer, the chimneys, and the bundle of toys in his famous poem "A Visit from Saint Nicholas." However, airborne Santa is a tough sell in New York. There aren't many working chimneys, so theoretically St. Nick needs to use the fire escape or get a master key from the superintendent. The reindeer would have to land between satellite dishes and water tanks. For all that effort his snack is going to be a hotdog and pineapple juice from Gray's Papaya or else almond milk and carob cookies.

Santa's trademark red suit with white collar and cuffs was created in the nineteenth century by Thomas Nast, a New York cartoonist for *Harper's Weekly* magazine. In addition to starting the tradition of extravagant holiday window displays, Macy's department store further jollied up Nast's image of Santa Claus. And if anyone was still doubting Santa's existence by then, the issue was put to rest once and for all when eight-year-old Virginia O'Hanlon wrote to the *New York Sun* from her home on West 95th Street in Manhattan to ask if Santa was real. On September 12, 1897, veteran newsman Francis Pharcellus Church replied in no uncertain terms, "Yes, VIRGINIA, there is a Santa Claus. He exists as certainly as love and generosity and devotion exist, and you know that they abound and give to your life its highest beauty and joy. Alas! how dreary would be the world if there were no Santa Claus." As for Virginia, she earned a master's degree from Columbia University, a doctorate from Fordham University, and went on to become an educator and school administrator.

Finally, along came poor Rudolph, the alternatively nosed ninth reindeer. He was created in 1939 by Robert L. May, a New York–born advertising copywriter for retailer Montgomery Ward, as part of a Christmas coloring book. And while "White Christmas" might be about spending the holiday in sunny California, the song was written by Israel Isidore Beilin, who moved with his family from Russia to New York's Lower East Side when he was five years old and later changed his name to Irving Berlin. In the 1947 perennial Christmas favorite *Miracle on 34th Street* the real Santa has to step in because the one playing him in the Macy's Parade is drunk. In a typical New York twist, the real Santa Claus must undergo a psychological evaluation in order to prove his credentials and avoid being committed to Bellevue Hospital. This was several years before the invention of antipsychotic drugs.

Happily, churches and community centers provide plenty of good music throughout the holidays, most of it at no cost. Otherwise, free-range caroling is a challenge in New York. Apartment dwellers think you're trying to deck the halls with take-out menus. Since 9/11,

big signs in the subway say, "If you see something, say something."
The Boston Marathon bombing confirmed the fact that it's now up to
the populace to catch terrorists. Imagine looking out your window and
spying people ganged together wearing wool hats, chanting from little
books, singing praise to God. I hope they know the words to "Police
Navidad." It'd be better for them to haul their holiday self-expression
off to a karaoke bar.

New Yorkers try to embrace the holidays by removing their black
Christmas and Hanukkah sweaters from the oven. However, it's stress-
ful knowing that you won't get another cab until after New Year's Eve
and that buying a tube of toothpaste will mean standing in line for an
hour. Advent, the traditional December holiday season, means "something about to arrive." It's about waiting. We are indeed accustomed to
waiting for subways and buses to arrive, traffic lights to change, and
food delivery (unless it's Asian), but so as not to punish locals, I've
long been an advocate of express lines in December for those buying
staples such as juice and toilet paper on the way home from work.
Also, just as Amtrak and Metro-North have "quiet cars," there could be
special subway cars to separate tired working stiffs from excessively
cheerful tourists and showgoers gleefully swinging oversize shopping
bags and loudly humming "The Carol of the Bells." This would go far
in fighting "holiday rage." As the curmudgeon H. L. Mencken so deli-
cately put it, "People say we need religion when what they really mean
is we need police."

New Year's Eve is, of course, when the ball drops and hordes of
out-of-towners stand freezing in Times Square. Many large cities offer
free public transportation on subways, buses, and commuter railroads
on New Year's Eve in an effort to discourage drunk driving. New York
experimented with free rides from eight p.m. to eight a.m. in 1984 and
1985, and the result was a surge in muggings, attempted stabbings, vandalism, and disorderly displays involving public intoxication. Roving
bands of teens designated the subway cars as their pop-up party sites,
and this further increased the number of felonies and arrests. Nowadays
the thinking is that if you can afford to go out on New Year's Eve, then
you can afford to go home. Which leads us to my favorite joke. Two

fleas leave Times Square after watching the ball drop. One flea says to the other, "Should we walk or take a dog?"

As for Presidents' Day, what better way to honor the founders of our country than go to Macy's or Bloomingdales and buy linens on sale? Unitarian Universalists are trying to have "Founding Fathers" changed to "Founding Parents," as we know a number of women did some of the heavy lifting (aka "womanual labor") behind the scenes. We considered fighting for "Founding Persons" but we're also engaged in trying to get "person" changed to "perself" to render it completely gender neutral.

Over the years it has come to my attention that people born on Christmas Eve and Christmas Day are often called Holly, Noel, or Carol. I'm just putting it out there that perhaps children born on Presidents' Day weekend could be named after linens, for example, Percale, Satin, Flannel, and Duvet. And why not call children born on Arbor Day Birch, Spruce, Sycamore, and Flowering Dogwood?

Thanksgiving is actually the perfect New York holiday. There are no religious obligations and it's all about excess. Even the food is stuffed with food. If you don't feel like cooking, the Chinese restaurants are open for business so the only kitchen accidents to watch out for are paper cuts. It's amazing how much General Tso's chicken tastes like turkey.

Chapter 18

HUMIDITY CITY

There are two basic seasons in New York: Influenza and Allergy. Obviously, the flu is going to find a happy home since public transportation is like a giant kindergarten with too many shared surfaces, too much close contact, and not enough coughing into elbows. It also doesn't help to go from frigid streets into apartment buildings with antiquated heating systems that are "regulated" by opening and closing the windows to allow the cold air from outside to reduce the Arizona-dry prison climate on the inside. The bed of the average New Yorker usually has a window slightly above the pillow and a radiator slightly below the pillow, which either results in bronchitis or one heck of an immune system. My father's bed was in exactly this position, and the man was never sick a day in his life. He didn't even have a doctor. He also used to swim in the Hudson River as a boy, so it's safe to assume he'd already been exposed to a little bit of everything by the time he got his army vaccinations.

Summer colds are also popular, especially when going from 95 degrees outdoors to subarctic office buildings and then down onto blistering subway platforms. These become incinerators where lifeless baked air is trapped underground only to be rearranged when a train arrives, pushing ahead of it a tremendous blast of even hotter, fustier air that's been roasting in a tunnel. Then you step into a subway car the temperature of a meat locker. Fortunately, there's a homeopathic cure for the ills induced by rapid cycling between shiver and swelter – liquor stores put containers of airplane-size vodka on the counter and label them "Flu Shots."

Logic suggests that the concrete jungle would be a safe haven for allergy sufferers. Au contraire. A recent Finnish study says that we city dwellers are more allergic because our urban setting lacks biodiversity. Another problem is our trees. In the early 1900s, the most popular tree planted was the American elm, which shed little pollen. These were killed by Dutch elm disease in the middle of the last century and replaced by several species of trees to which many people are highly allergic. That's because street trees are chosen for their resistance to disease, insects and drought, and their ability to withstand smog. Basically, city planners take the size, shape, color, and hardiness of the trees into account but not their deleterious effects on about 40 percent of the inhabitants.

What passes for winter in New York is rather laughable to a native Buffalonian. I doubt that my Wall Street colleagues had ever hoarded Wonder Bread bags as kids so they could place them between sock and boot (two on each foot) before heading outside. Still, a few inches of well-placed snow and a couple of fallen tree limbs can practically shut this city down. Newscasters love working themselves and everyone else into a frenzy over approaching storms. They go into grocery stores and film shoppers stocking up on a month's worth of milk and eggs (largely because the customers panicked after watching the storm coverage on TV). Then the TV cameras go to the Sanitation Department where big, shiny plows are ready to rumble and the road salt is piled high. If only the plows were fitted to move all the parked cars that will be abandoned on the streets and make snow removal nearly impossible.

There are a few New Yorkers who've been keeping cross-country skis hidden away for just such an occasion and head straight up Fifth Avenue early in the morning and into Central Park. The snow accumulates so rarely and space is at such a premium that many city kids don't have sleds, so they use garbage can lids or lunch trays or, they wrap cardboard in a Hefty bag. For a few hours the Frozen Apple becomes a winter wonderland. Then it quickly descends into a slush nightmare, with street corners that require hip waders to navigate deceptively monstrous puddles and sidewalks heaped with enough superstrength rock salt to vaporize a medium-size goldendoodle compliments of lawsuit-fearing business owners.

Jerry Seinfeld once quipped, "My parents didn't want to move to Florida, but they turned sixty and that's the law." Miami is often called the last stop on the Long Island Rail Road. When New Yorkers move to the Land of Milk of Magnesia they can become sullen, since there's not as much to complain about as they sit there eating early-bird specials of skinless, boneless chicken. Their adult children can sometimes be circumspect when it comes to saying the winter is mild in New York, for fear that the parents will return early from the Old Country, aka West Palm Beach.

Spring means that Central Park becomes a dreamscape of frothy pink-and-white blossoms that make the trees look as if they've been decorated with scoops of ice cream. The streets fill with babies and puppies. At my Unitarian Universalist (UU) church, my pew mate Mary-Ella and I always make a wager on how many Easter hats we'll see. Between ten and twenty is usually a good guess. However, some devout Yankee fan usually rocks up in a baseball cap and we're never sure how to count that.

Daylight saving time is always an adventure in New York. Fortunately, the UUs have a long coffee hour ("coffee cacophony" is more like it) following the service, and in the spring, everyone who forgot to switch their clocks and missed the service can walk directly into that gathering without being too embarrassed. The real problem is in the autumn, when the people who were planning on just going to coffee hour arrive an hour early and end up having to actually attend the service first.

With regard to the trains, most local service providers, such as the Long Island Rail Road, enter the Twilight Zone during the autumn daylight saving changeover. For instance, if your LIRR train leaves Penn Station at 1:19 a.m. and is supposed to arrive at Plandome at 2 a.m., it will arrive at 1 a.m. That's no inconvenience for the customer. However, riders on Amtrak might be surprised to find that trains heading to and from the city stop in their tracks, so to speak, during the autumn changeover, entering into a state of suspended animation. At two a.m., Amtrak trains stop and wait an hour for the new two a.m., assuming they were running on time to begin with, which is a big assumption when it comes to Amtrak. As for the subway, those operators needn't worry about such things since they're not foolish enough to commit to a schedule in the first place.

It's true enough that I arrived in New York City in the dead of winter and considered it to be a big joke, but I was not prepared for the summer by a long shot. Buffalo has never even recorded a temperature of 100 degrees or higher with nearby Lake Erie acting as a gigantic air-conditioner. If the mercury did rise to slightly uncomfortable levels during the day it usually cooled down substantially by nightfall. Chocolate didn't melt in our hands to begin with so we wondered why the makers of M&M's had to guarantee that theirs wouldn't. This just wasn't a problem. And Buffalonians think that all Dairy Queens are closed from October until May. Who goes out for a Blizzard in a blizzard?

It's officially summer in New York City when you see the newspaper picture or TV footage of kids frolicking in the spray of an open fire hydrant, usually in Harlem or Brooklyn. Soon to follow are the power failures that occur as cranked-up air-conditioners overtax the power grid and too many New Yorkers simultaneously research their cold and allergy symptoms on WebMD.

As summer progresses and the city seems to be slipping toward the equator, the homicide rate always rises. The tabloids like to correlate this to a spike in the consumption of ice cream since Mister Softee sales rise in tandem with stabbings and gunshots. It's surprising that local weather forecasters haven't added this Ice Cream Indicator to their tracking of the heat index and the pollen count. However, the police call the rise in murders the "Are you lookin' at me?" effect from the movie *Taxi Driver*, which was shot during a New York summer heat wave (and its fraternal twin, the garbage strike). In hot weather people go out more, congregate more, and tempers flare. Most of the violence takes place when the temperature is in the low- to mid-90s. After the mercury creeps past 97 degrees, the murder rate drops precipitously. Apparently there is such a thing as too hot to kill. I once saw a T-shirt that said, "Here Today, Gone to Maui." New York should sell ones that say "Too Hot for Homicide."

Alfred Hitchcock's murder mystery *Rear Window* depicts New York during a heat wave. Actor Jimmy Stewart solves a crime by spying on his neighbors out of his tenement-building window. Which begs the question, do New Yorkers really use telescopes to peer into other apartments? Yes, but all they usually see are the flickering lights of computer screens as people research diets on the Internet while eating Funyuns.

By the third day of a heat wave the entire city begins to smell like pee and one understands why the musical *Urinetown* was such a hit in New York. When it finally starts to rain one assumes the pee smell will be washed away, but for at least a day after a good downpour the city only smells more like pee.

Throughout the sulking haze of a heat wave, air-conditioners remain on high, the power grid hovers near collapse, and blackouts are always a possibility. This is particularly bad for politicians if elections are looming because you can't be sure whether you're going to get the Bad Blackout of 1977, when the knives came out and looters were looting other looters, or the Good Blackout of 2003, when neighbors helped one another, citizens voluntarily went into the streets to direct traffic, and people had parties where they pooled and then barbecued all their perishables. Whereas most disasters result in a baby boom nine months later, people were so busy out helping one another there was actually a dip in births following the Good Blackout of 2003. As it happens, New York has just one electric company – Con Edison. And it advertises on TV because why? If we're dissatisfied are we going to switch to using treadmill power or candlelight or night vision goggles? Meantime, we pay for their service while they try and frighten us into doing all the work. Signs in the subway say: "You thought they reported the gas leak. They thought you did." Add your own scary music soundtrack.

How to beat the heat is a common topic of conversation during stifling, humid New York summers. As with restaurants, doctors, and travel routes, everyone seems to have an opinion. In the old days before air-conditioning, people slept on fire escapes and rooftops, and whole families would decamp for the night to public parks. Nowadays, people take refuge in such places as the M5 bus, rumored to be the coldest; the freezer section of Fairway Market; the chilled penguin house at the Central Park Zoo; the New York Public Library; and the Metropolitan Museum of Art (paintings need climate control just like humans). Movie theaters tend to be 40 degrees and so they're a cool haven so long as you plan for pneumonia afterward. Some intrepid New Yorkers set up beach chairs in air-conditioned twenty-four-hour ATM lobbies with their laptops and ear buds. There's always the old standby of catching a breeze on the Staten Island Ferry, which is *free*. It was the Staten Island Ferry that Edna St. Vincent Millay was celebrating in her poem "Recuerdo" with the lines:

We were very tired, we were very merry –
We had gone back and forth all night on the ferry.

To fight droughts, mayors try with varying degrees of success to get New Yorkers to use less water. During one protracted dry spell a frustrated Mayor Bloomberg attempted to make it illegal to wash vehicles, sidewalks, and driveways. Most famously, Mayor Koch endeavored to limit toilet flushing during a 1980s drought with the ditty, "If it's yellow, let it mellow; if it's brown, flush it down!" But then he had a flair for publicity. It was said that if they could keep a camera on Mayor Koch in the operating room he would never die.

Flu is the third leading cause of death after heart disease and cancer. But most New Yorkers who eat out regularly contract food poisoning at least once a year. The old saw goes, "Never eat seafood in a month without an R in it." However, my mother the nurse likes to raise the bar by saying, "Don't eat seafood unless you can see the body of water it came from out the restaurant window."

What happens when single people without relatives nearby or health insurance fall ill? That's where Chinese restaurants come in handy. The patient simply orders white rice, egg drop soup, and plain steamed chicken off the diet section of the menu, and ginger ale. No one on a diet orders from the diet menu in Chinese restaurants. It's just a euphemism for "deathly ill and housebound." Miso soup and edamame from the Japanese restaurant are also good medicine, but steer clear of the wasabi, which is Japanese for "put the toilet paper in the fridge."

Cockroaches are known to carry a number of disease-causing bacteria including salmonella and streptococcus, in addition to being a source of asthma and allergies, especially in children. I never saw what's known as a "common cockroach" until I moved to New York City. Western New York's official scary bug is the silverfish, a wingless silvery-gray insect that likes to slither out from underneath cans when you least expect it. New Yorkers don't complain about roaches. The roaches were here before us and they'll be here after us just like the dedicated perfume sprayers at Bloomingdale's. We're used to putting everything in the fridge, from cereal boxes and crackers to candy and chips. The American cockroach, which New Yorkers call a "water bug" in order to distinguish between the two in all our vermin stories, looks like a common cockroach on steroids, and no matter how many times I see one and remind myself it's not an attack animal, it scares the bejesus out of me.

New York no longer gets hit by plagues, but it still has plenty of rats and mice. There's a reason every store keeps a cat in the basement. Bodega and deli owners would rather clean a litter box and be fined by the Health Department than have their entire inventory gnawed and consumed without payment.

Chapter 19

TAILS OF NEW YORK

After his handling of 9/11, Rudy Giuliani is probably best known for making the fur fly over pet ferrets by banning them as a health threat. He made it clear that ferret enthusiasts (or "people obsessed with weasels" in his words) should get help because it's "a sickness." If anything suspicious ever befalls him the investigation will surely start in the shadowy subterranean world of contraband ferrets, which are allowed in New York State but outlawed in New York City. Oddly, keeping chickens, bees, and pigeons is perfectly legal in all five boroughs.

Pigeons are famously the bane and mascot of New York City. They arrived with the colonists in the 1600s and likewise succeeded in putting down roots and flourishing. There have been pigeon supporters and pigeon detractors ever since. Pigeon raisers, racers, feeders, and rescuers are constantly pitted against pigeon relocators, cullers, sterilizers, and eaters. Building owners erect owl statues, netting, and metal spikes to keep these resilient birds from fouling public spaces. The Metropolitan Transit Authority has tried zapping pigeons with electrical wire, not enough to kill them, but enough to keep them from spattering outdoor subway stations. Pigeons appear to be with us for the long haul, despite the rumor that you never see any baby pigeons. They do not spring to life fully formed, but are very clever at hiding their young, notwithstanding what appears to be a lazy lifestyle of drunkenly weaving through traffic to forage for pizza crusts, French fries, and bagel crumbs. As for the romantic notion that pigeons mate for life, some do, but like most New Yorkers, they tend to stay together until one finds a better mate. Being an urban pigeon is no walk in the park.

It turns out that it's not just the coupling and uncoupling of New York young people that makes for popular story fodder. *And Tango Makes Three* is a 2005 children's book based on the romance between two male chinstrap penguins living in the Central Park Zoo. Roy and Silo were behaving as a couple, made a nest together, and attempted to hatch a rock. When a male-female couple produced two eggs and couldn't care for both, zookeepers gave one to Roy and Silo. The female chick was named "Tango." However, the book relating this story was immediately controversial because Tango had two daddies, and numerous attempts have been made to ban it from bookshelves. Conservatives may not have succeeded in their censorship campaign, but they were surely delighted when Silo was hit with the six-year itch and took up with a female from the West Coast named Scrappy. This sudden change in partners "rocked the gay world," reported influential commentator Andrew Sullivan.

Further exotica is in the air with the thousand or so monk parakeets that have built colonies throughout the five boroughs. The ancestors of these birds were imported to JFK Airport in crates from South America in order to become pets, but they skipped immigration altogether. Like most things in New York, these upstarts are both loved and loathed. Some residents adore their vibrant colors and cheerful chirping, while others have classified them as a nuisance since they build nests around heat-emitting transformers atop utility poles, which then catch fire. You can probably guess on which side of this debate Con Edison falls.

Petworking: When your social circle and work opportunities come almost entirely from the people you've met through your "animal companions." Despite the fact that locals love to complain, fewer than one in five New Yorkers vote, compared to more than half of the folk in the rest of New York State and slightly under half in the rest of the country. However, one in three owns a pet.

Then there are the less common animals that are more common than you might think in our urban jungle. Elusive coyotes and swooping red-tailed hawks have taken up residence in Central Park. Zelda, the wild turkey named after F. Scott Fitzgerald's wife, blithely struts about Battery Park uncooked, occasionally visiting TriBeCa and Greenwich Village. A poisonous Egyptian cobra that may or may not have escaped from the Bronx Zoo managed to keep up a weeklong Twitter feed about her adventures. A three-foot corn snake popped up in a Bronx man's nineteenth-floor apartment. Four intrepid Brooklyn women found a python in their home, packed it up in a pillowcase, hopped on the G train, and delivered it to an animal rescue center. Around the holidays it's possible to see the three camels that star (as themselves) in the *Radio City Christmas Spectacular* walking down 51st Street.

Then there was the 500-pound tiger kept as a pet in a tiny Harlem high-rise apartment that turned on its owner, Antoine Yates. Yates checked into a hospital saying that he'd been attacked by a pit bull. Animal Control was sent for the tiger while Yates was convicted of keeping dangerous animals in the city and given a prison term. Yates commented: "Ironically we were both placed in cages for the first time." After serving five months in jail, Yates sued New York City and Police Department for searching his home without a warrant, the loss of his pets, and $7,000 he claimed had been stolen. U.S. District judge Sidney Stein dismissed the case saying that Yates was full of chutzpah.

That alligators dwell in the sewers is a popular urban legend, along with buried treasure on Liberty Island and a ghost ship on the Hudson River. Except that alligators *have* been found in city sewers and storm drains. A two-foot caiman (a species of crocodile) played hide-and-seek with pursuers for a week in Central Park in 2001 until alligator wranglers were brought up from Florida. The parks commissioner designated the reptile "Damon the Caiman." A four-foot crocodile was found wandering around a Queens park in 2003 but wisely turned himself in to the responding police officers. It's possible to view and photograph a subterranean gator at the 14th Street/Eighth Avenue subway station where a fanciful bronze sculpture by Tom Otterness depicts an alligator emerging from a manhole cover and biting the backside of a person with a money-bag head. (That urban myth out of the way, I've never seen anyone fry an egg on the sidewalk, even during the worst heat wave.)

Like most urban dwellers, New Yorkers gravitate toward cats and dogs when it comes to house pets. Even if pet owners see one another in the park every day they tend to call each other after the pet, for example, Penny's mom or Buber's dad. On the Upper West Side in the 1980s I knew a golden retriever named Freud, a Collie named Manic, a high-strung Yorkie called Schizo, a teacup poodle named Crackers, and a tabby cat called Tofu.

New Yorkers tend to have pets instead of kids. Space is limited and it's perfectly legal to sell or give away the offspring of your dog or cat. As a result, lots of businesses have sprung up to pamper these beloved pooches and pussycats. There's doggy daycare, clothing boutiques, pet-icures, holiday photos, Zen classes, and party planners who will throw a splendid Bark Mitzvah. Prospect Park in Brooklyn is home to Dog Beach, where pups of all breeds and sizes can frolic together and perfect their doggy paddle. On the medical front you can get hydrotherapy, acupuncture, aromatherapy, and of course psychotherapy. Then there's dog yoga, which is called (what else?) doga. Let's just say that no one here was surprised when New York businesswoman Leona Helmsley left $12 million to her Maltese named Trouble, which handlers were always supposed to refer to as "Princess" rather than "the dog."

One study says that two out of three New Yorkers talk to their pets over the phone. If all the pets in New York find out they're adopted on the same day the crisis hotlines will be overflowing. Don't get me wrong, I love animals and have four dogs of my own. However, I think one has to accept the fact that they're a mixed bag. If I pass out in the apartment they'll bark and whine for help, and perhaps the spaniel will try the phone. But after a few days they'll eat me.

The professional dog walker leading a pack of sixteen or so canines to a park is another must-get NYC photo, complete with Labrador retrievers (who already have waterproof coats) dressed in Gucci rain gear. Although you may want to wait until winter when the Pugz (Ugg boots for dogs) come out. Interestingly, I've heard more than one person comment that the dog walkers look happier than the nannies.

New York seems to be the capital of the three-legged dog. I guess the prevailing attitude is that if we can tough it out in this city on two legs, our pets can certainly manage on three.

Chapter 20

WALL STREET BULL

What's known as the Battery at the tip of Manhattan is named for the artillery batteries there that protected the original trading post. This is where Homeland Security originated in the 1600s. The construction of the Battery was followed by the building of a wall by Dutch settlers to protect against a British invasion and attacks by Native Americans, the outline of which is now Wall Street. After the English prevailed, the inhabitants began moving their residences northward in large numbers while continuing to do business in what would become known as downtown Manhattan, and eventually the financial center of the country.

Why did I decide to go to Wall Street in the early 1980s? It was true I had no money, but stocks were still in the doldrums and it didn't appear to be a place of opportunity. What intrigued me about the markets was probability. As an only child and an only grandchild with no cousins, my mother, father, aunt, and uncle played poker at family gatherings. Even when I was five years old they had no interest in Candy Land, Chutes and Ladders, or I Spy. So I was perched atop a couple of phone books dealing seven-card stud at midnight calling, "One-eyed jacks are wild" and telling the person to my right to "cut 'em thin and win" or "slice 'em deep and weep." Had I offered the cut to the person on my left they would've screamed at me since you never give the first card to the person who cut the deck, and poker is dealt left to right. In other words, those vultures didn't give me any breaks for not yet having started first grade. And we played for money. My piggy bank could empty or fill with enough for a new tricycle in one night of cards.

In no time I became intrigued by other games of strategy and probability such as chess, backgammon, and blackjack. By middle school I was riding my bicycle over the Peace Bridge to the Fort Erie Race Track in Canada and handicapping the horses. It was hard to pay attention to math lessons in school, but when the objective was winning a game or betting to make money it turned out I could compute probabilities in my head all day long. Games of probability (as opposed to chance) meant taking a bunch of facts and determining what was the most likely outcome in any given situation. So when I first read about stock options, they were no different to me than all the other games I loved, only on Wall Street I wouldn't have to sit inside a smoky casino and worry about getting thrown out for counting cards, which is perfectly legal but frowned upon, especially by the burly men who were threatening to kick me out.

Much like the sitcom *Will & Grace* is credited with helping to recognize the equality of same-sex marriage, the sitcom *Family Ties* presaged the great bull market of the 1980s. The family's oldest child, Alex P. Keaton, played by Michael J. Fox, rejected his parents' hippiedom with quotes like, "People who have money don't need people." And no one summed up the decade's confluence of racism, classism, politics, and greed better than Tom Wolfe in his 1987 *Bonfire of the Vanities*. Meantime, the movie *Wall Street* had its chief market manipulator Gordon Gekko famously declare that "greed, for lack of a better word, is good." Jerry Sterner's play *Other People's Money* featured a successful corporate raider called "Larry the Liquidator," who becomes rich gobbling up companies and selling off their assets by using a computer stock-analyzing program.

The bull began a big run when the galloping inflation of the 1970s and early 1980s subsided and economic growth returned. The real estate and stock markets soared, along with employment, and when interest rates declined there was easy lending. Every financially struggling individual was suddenly preapproved for a dozen credit cards. In short, the cliffs and canyons of Wall Street became the site of a modern-day gold rush with the prospect of easy money pulsating in the air like Michael Jackson's hit song "Beat It."

While New York's homeless population went unchecked, a class of nouveau riche sprang up wearing designer clothes, driving imported cars, bidding up artwork, and attending $1,000-a-plate fundraisers. These impetuous young entrepreneurs and extravagant consumers so defined the new era that *Newsweek* magazine declared 1984 "The Year of the Yuppie." (The inevitable backlash, much of which was aimed at those engaged in neighborhood gentrification, would involve "Die Yuppie Scum" T-shirts, protest signs, and graffiti.)

Big egos emerged to go along with the gold collar pins propping up wide red ties, Mabe pearl earrings, and pointy-toed shoes with spiky colored heels. Real estate prices skyrocketed. New York State's first "parking garage car condominium" opened up in Park Slope, Brooklyn, with spots selling for $29,000 in addition to a monthly maintenance fee of $142.66. New York suddenly exemplified the tale of two cities, with street people sleeping in the doorways of multimillion-dollar Park Avenue penthouses. Unlike the gated communities and exclusive enclaves typically inhabited by suburban financiers and socialites, in New York City splendor and squalor have a history of presenting themselves side by side. Legions of homeless people were occupying the Financial District's Zuccotti Park, formerly called Liberty Plaza Park, long before the Occupy Wall Street protesters.

An endless game of cat and mouse emerged between insider traders and law enforcement that would result in more than a few prison terms and political careers. Most notably, federal prosecutor Rudy Giuliani on his path to becoming mayor of New York City (1994–2001) popularized the perp walk for white-collar criminals such as Ivan Boesky (the real-life model for Gordon Gekko) and Junk Bond King Michael Milken. Giuliani's trajectory is even more remarkable when you consider that his father served time in the maximum-security prison Sing Sing for assault and robbery.

I began my Wall Street career in January of 1984, which, unbeknownst to me, just happened to be the beginning of the biggest bull market in history. It was a time when middle-class individuals started investing in stocks, an arena that had largely been the preserve of people with family fortunes or else high incomes. This would spawn numerous TV shows and even entire networks devoted to the markets. It was also go time for M&A mavens, hedge fund managers, investment bankers, arbitrageurs, corporate raiders, entrepreneurs, and, as it would turn out, more than a few Ponzi scheme operators. My company made a primary market in what are called derivative products. In our case this meant options based on a basket of stocks (or index) that had a high correlation with the Dow Jones Industrial Average. So it was necessary to determine which way the entire market was headed from moment to moment and protect (hedge) our positions by trading other derivative products.

I quickly became familiar with big market movers, such as leveraged buyouts, and financial strategies, which included greenmail, hired guns, white squires, poison pills, tender offers, toehold purchases, painting the tape, triple witching hour, front running, bottom feeding, leveraging up, averaging down, takeovers, reverse takeovers, amalgamations, bootstrap acquisitions, backward integration, cashing out, short squeezes, dawn raids, random walkers, Godfather offers, the Pac-Man defense, sandbagging, sleeping beauties, summer soldiers, supermajority amendments, knights that could be white, gray, or black, golden parachutes, and golden handshakes. These were different from the gold diggers who could be found at the local watering holes in high heels and short skirts starting around five p.m. When it came to terminology, the animal kingdom was subject to heavy play. There were bull runs, bear raids, bear hugs, greedy pigs, dogs with fleas, sheep to slaughter, black swan events, Fed hawks and doves, ostriches with heads in the sand, wolves on the prowl, killer bees, stool pigeons, porcupine provisions, dead cat bounces, lobster traps, shark repellent, crocodile tears, and penguins left huddled together for warmth.

As it turned out, most *Animal Farm* references were not inappropriate since some animals were indeed more equal than others, at least when it came to the possession of information. Atlantic City was much fairer in that all blackjack players, including the dealer, had the same data available to them, and in Atlantic City when you lost you were still given free drinks, a hotel room, and a limousine ride home. Instead of the famous bronze statue of the *Charging Bull* in Bowling Green Park near Wall Street, with its testicles aglow from being rubbed by thousands of desperate hands, they might want to build another memorial called The Tomb of the Unknown Investor, symbolizing all those who've been defeated by the marketplace. Shady stockbrokers were known for always using credit cards that gave free miles so it was easy to flee the country once the cards were all maxed out and the game was over.

Traders had catchy everyday expressions such as "The trend is your friend," "They're crying, I'm buying," "An object in motion tends to stay in motion," " Keep it simple stupid (KISS)," "What goes up must come down," "Don't try to catch a falling knife," "Don't fight the Fed," "When there's nothing to do, do nothing," "Buy on rumor, sell on news," and "No one ever went broke ringing the cash register." Wall Street bosses loved to say to young dumb employees, "Do you want the short answer or the long answer?" The short answer was, "No way." The long answer was, of course, "No fucking way." There were no swear jars in the Financial District that I was aware of.

My favorite bit of expert financial advice was that if you wanted to double your money fast then you should fold it in half. Wall Streeters need a sense of invincibility and are therefore terrific self-diagnosers and self-medicators. Dismissing pain was also popular, like it was with coaches who'd instruct me and my teammates to "walk off" a shattered pelvis or collapsed lung.

A friend on the stock exchange, whom I'll call Nate Goldberg, was having horrible abdominal pains but wouldn't go to a doctor. Nate had grown up an Orthodox Jew in Brooklyn, where his father was a rabbi and his mother was, well, his Mother. Nate's mother kept calling her son's apartment like a telemarketer on crack to insist that he see a doctor. He stopped answering the phone. Then there was a knock at his apartment door. Nate was in too much pain to rise from his chair. "Who is it?" yelled Nate. "Mr. Goldberg, your mother called us from Brooklyn and we're here to take you to the hospital. Open the door." It was the Hatzolah, the volunteer emergency medical service supported by Jewish communities. "Go away!" shouted Nate. "Mr. Goldberg, if you don't open the door we'll break it down." "You're not allowed to do that," replied Nate. "Yes, we can. Your mother said you are trying to harm yourself." Nate opened the door. They rushed him to the nearest hospital. His appendix had burst. In another hour he would've been dead. Nate later said it was the biggest "I told you so" in Jewish history. But the story gets better. Nate's parents had wanted him to be a rabbi, but he'd become a trader and married a shiksa ballerina. They'd had a son together who was now nineteen, and his parents didn't know about the marriage or their grandson. When Nate woke up after the operation he saw his parents, his ex-wife, and his son all standing over him. He screamed for the nurse and asked for morphine – lots and lots of morphine.

Working on the trading floor not only led to elevated idiocy levels, but also hearing loss and throat polyps. To be understood above the din we enhanced our continuous shouting with hand signals that were based on American Sign Language. In addition to confirming prices (fifteen and fifty sound a lot alike across a loud, crowded, caffeinated room) the hand signals were good for ordering lunch and telling someone you were making a quick dash for the lav, which was signed as "M-E" for "medical emergency," since stepping away from the trading pit for even a second could be hazardous to your financial health. Best of all, no one could beat a team of traders with the secret weapon of sign language when it came to playing charades at parties.

Then there was the additional stress from the dozens of practical jokes played on a daily basis. One trader made a ritual of going to near-by Brooks Brothers and picking out a new hat at the beginning of every quarter. A couple of colleagues went to the store and bought the same hat in a half size larger and a half size smaller. They let him wear the new hat for a few days and then substituted it for the smaller one. After a few more days they swapped it for the larger hat. The next day their pal didn't show up for work. Or the next day. They called his house and his wife said he'd checked himself into the hospital because his head was "expanding and contracting" and he was certain that he had a brain tumor. Fortunately, no brain surgery was performed and a "watch and wait" approach was adopted, part of which involved the man measuring the circumference of his head every day and charting any sudden changes. A similar prank was pulled on a floor broker with a knee injury. He was getting around using a metal cane. One of his partners would shave an inch off the cane every afternoon while he was filing tickets in the booth. After a week of cane cutting the injured party went to his doctor and said he felt like he was sinking on the *Titanic*.

Ahead of the game or behind, eventually it comes time to get out. Shouting in a loud trading pit all day is not the best thing for one's health, as evidenced by all those who've had heart attacks, bleeding ulcers, acid reflux, migraines, hypertension, insomnia, looked twice their age, or were repeatedly packed off to rehab. If your job requires that a defibrillator be installed three feet away, it's something to think about. After five years on the floor of the stock exchange I decided to see what else the city had to offer.

It's worth noting that along with the great bull market came a decline in the quality of students studying medicine, engineering, education, criminal justice, social work, agriculture, and forestry (money doesn't grow on trees, just hedge funds). Suddenly, everyone wanted finance degrees and MBAs. The next best moneymaker was being a quantitative analyst ("quant") or computer programmer. It's a shame that the appeal of Wall Street prevented other important areas of study from engaging many of those young minds with a passion and a talent for them. On second thought, without all those techies we might not have the social network game FarmVille, where you can spend hours plowing fake land, planting fake seeds, growing fake crops, and raising fake livestock.

Chapter 21

SECTS AND THE CITY

The New Netherland colonists were given freedom to worship in private from the get-go, despite occasional interference from various directors and clergymen. Religious tolerance expanded under English rule, though the residents had inherited some anti-Catholicism and anti-Semitism from their parents. It was a mostly Protestant group, but also home to the oldest Jewish congregation in the United States, dating to 1654. When Anne Hutchinson was banished from New England for questioning Puritan practices, she headed to the more tolerant New Netherland. For people who had left Europe to escape religious intolerance, the Pilgrims were rather a my-way-or-the-highway kind of sect when it came to creeds.

Today, New York is often called the Secular City, and has even been accused of suffering from an "over-separation of church and state" because of a rule that bans organized worship in city school buildings even when no students are using them.

Capitalism and religion have mostly cohabited happily in New York City over the centuries. In fact, the architect James Renwick Jr. designed both St. Patrick's Cathedral and the former facade of the New York Stock Exchange. St. Patrick's Cathedral, at 50th and Fifth Avenue, is the neo-Gothic home of the archbishop of New York. Completed in 1878, it is the center of the oldest Roman Catholic parish in the city. St. Patrick was chosen as patron of the cathedral because 100,000 Irish immigrants had already flooded the city by 1842, and the Potato

Famine (1845–1852) brought another 200,000. By 1860, of the roughly 1 million people living in New York, one-fifth were Irish, and by 1869 New York contained more Irish than Dublin.

Hundreds of thousands of people now come to see the Nativity scene at St. Patrick's at Christmastime. In 2011, visitors were treated to a small miracle when a statue of a golden retriever popped up between the donkey and the cow, a likeness to the one owned by the monsignor in charge of setting up the crèche. The official comment from the church was that it would be logical for the shepherds to bring some of their sheep and a sheepdog to meet the baby Jesus.

Speaking of church rituals, it should be noted that smoke coming out of a New York chimney has nothing to do with electing a new pope. It's usually just investment bankers and hedge fund managers burning their diaries and deal memos.

In response to the construction of the Catholic cathedral, the Episcopal Diocese of New York decided to build one of its own on Amsterdam Avenue at 112th Street. The plans called for St. John the Divine to be the world's largest cathedral, and construction was started in 1892. But after 120 years the cathedral remains incomplete (and in need of renovations) and is therefore often called St. John the Unfinished. As a result of its long gestation, there's a jumble (fusion?) of architectural styles, including French Gothic, English Gothic, Spanish Gothic, Gothic Revival, Romanesque, Renaissance, Norman, and Byzantine.

Jews have the Romanesque Revival building that's home to Temple Emanu-El on Fifth Avenue at 65th Street, which is extolled for being one of the largest and most beautiful synagogues in the world. The current incarnation went up in 1929 on the site of the mansion once owned by Mrs. William B. Astor.

The first mosque in the city was the Islamic Cultural Center of New York on Third Avenue and 96th Street, which was completed in 1991. The building is rotated 29 degrees from the city's north-south street grid in order to be oriented toward Mecca, the birthplace of Muhammad.

Spiritual tourists may likewise find enlightenment visiting the Ganesha Hindu Temple in Flushing, Queens, where the list of services includes everything from holy baths to hair offerings. Or at Our Lady of Mount Carmel Grotto in Rosebank, Staten Island, which was designed and constructed by the local Italian-American community, and also serves as a convalescent home for previously venerated religious statuary. After 9/11 many residents left pictures and prayers here for their 274 lost loved ones.

In New York you can find every known religion, including Haitian Vodou, Kabbalah, Jainism, Santeria, Sufism, Bahá'í, and Jews for Jesus, along with the Church of Euthanasia ("Save the Planet, Kill Yourself"), the Church of the SubGenius (Paul Reubens aka Pee-wee Herman is a minister), the School of Kemetic Thought and Spirituality (if you get through the tapes and figure it out, let me know), and a handful of Marxist guerrillas. Churches throughout the city advertise services in dozens of languages, including Czech, Korean, Portuguese, Hungarian, Russian, Polish, Armenian, Arabic, and Creole. Likewise, various Buddhist temples offer services in Thai, Tibetan, Chinese, Spanish, Japanese, English, and Vietnamese. Teams of male Mormon missionaries encounter wisenheimer New Yorkers who ask which one is the designated driver and if they're planning to marry each other. And hipsters in Greenpoint, Brooklyn, do the Walk of Shame on Sunday mornings past legions of elderly Polish ladies heading for Mass.

It's because New York is so ecumenical that it can remain open 24 hours a day, 365 days a year. It's never everybody's holiday on any given day. If the Greek diners are closed for Christmas then the Indian restaurants are open. If the Italian restaurants are closed on Easter then the kosher delis are open. If the kosher delis are shuttered for Passover then the Persian restaurants are serving. If the Persian restaurants are closed for Ramadan then the Chinese restaurants are open. And if the Chinese restaurants are closed for … well, they're never closed, lucky for us. That's because Chinese restaurants don't serve breakfast and all the workers can sleep until eleven a.m. Despite the name, egg rolls aren't for breakfast.

In New York "evil-doers" aren't people working with international terrorist conspiracies but those who ruin your dry cleaning, hold the subway doors open so the train can't leave, and deliver your food cold.

And for some reason lots of Jewish people order from Chinese restaurants, but you never see Chinese people ordering from kosher restaurants. Maybe they should try offering matzo balls with fortunes inside.

Atheists in New York are actually quite busy, because in such a diverse place there are so many different gods not to believe in. However, it may not be a good idea to admit you're an atheist, not for fear of discrimination, but because everyone will ask you to cover for them at work since technically you don't get to take off for any religious holidays, and every day is somebody's holiday (refer back to the parking schedule). Then again, one might question the very existence of atheists in New York, at least ones with cars. Just like the old saying, "There are no atheists in foxholes," there are no atheists looking for parking places in New York. Prime spots have been known to generate believers the same way sharing the secret art of the MetroCard swipe with baffled tourists has made us all into Good Samaritans for at least one minute per week. New York is also home to a fair share of agnostics. They believe that if heaven and hell *do* exist then heaven is actually hotter because heat rises, except when it's been collecting on subway platforms.

Most Manhattan graveyards are either full up or built over, but the Bronx is home to the splendid 400-acre Woodlawn Cemetery. More like an outdoor museum, where visitors are welcome and tours are given, it's the final resting place of jazz greats Duke Ellington and Max Roach, composer Irving Berlin, and many other luminaries from all walks of life. Meantime, Brooklyn contains the picturesque Green-Wood Cemetery, home to Jean-Michael Basquiat, Leonard Bernstein, hotdog inventor Charles Feltman, and *New York Tribune* founder Horace Greeley (despite his advice to "Go West, young man"), along with a very much alive colony of colorful monk parakeets. A cemetery provision barring anyone who died in jail should have applied to notorious Tammany Hall leader "Boss" Tweed, who took his last breath while doing time for corruption in the Ludlow Street Jail (which had been built under his direction). But the Boss managed to sidestep the rules even in death, and his family was able to have him interred at Green-Wood. Legendary New York journalist Pete Hamill told a friend that he bought the plot next to Boss Tweed, and therefore a reporter will be keeping an eye on the political operator for eternity. The plot of sewing-machine inventor Elias Howe includes a grave for their family dog Fannie, who had "limpid eyes" according to the poetic epitaph.

Both cemeteries are nonsectarian, but they're also considered to be exclusive final resting grounds and therefore pricey. Like any good address in New York, a cemetery can be expensive even if you pass the screening committee. A priest friend gave me the suggestion that if you buy one plot, it's possible to return later with a big plant along with the ashes of any added family members and discreetly inter them yourself.

It comes as no surprise that Mayor Ed Koch wins the award for funeral irony. Born in New York to Jewish parents who emigrated from Poland, he's buried in a Christian cemetery in a largely Dominican neighborhood. And despite a penchant for shellfish, he certainly wasn't trying to "pass," since his headstone says the word *Jewish* four times. Perhaps most remarkably, the words "How'm I doin'?" do not appear once.

Still, as far as characters go, Damon Runyon may have surpassed Koch not only in life but in death. Runyon wrote sardonic but sentimental tales celebrating gamblers, gangsters, horse players, con artists, bootleggers, boxers, goldfish swallowers, swells, floozies, boozehounds, lowlifes, actors, and showgirls with nicknames such as Hymie Banjo Eyes, the Seldom Seen Kid, Sam the Gonoph, and Dream Street Rose. Runyon's stories were often based on real acquaintances and experiences, and two of them became the basis for the famous musical *Guys and Dolls*. When he died in 1946, the creator of so many colorful Broadway characters had his ashes (illegally) scattered over Times Square among all the hoofers and hustlers he'd immortalized.

A favorite joke in this city is that Jesus could've been a New Yorker – he lived at home into his thirties, worked in his father's business, walked everywhere, became a marketing guru, and his mother believed he was God. But seriously, it'd be hard to tell if Jesus were to choose New York for his return. There are so many long-haired dudes wearing sandals who are trying to build a following in this city. Plus, if you call out "Jesus" in a crowded place, a dozen heads will turn. New

York's strong feminist contingent argues that Jesus could've just as easily been a woman because he had to feed a crowd at a moment's notice, he was constantly talking to men who wouldn't listen, and even after he was dead there was still a ton of work to be done. These gals are certain the Wise Men weren't women or else they'd have brought along gifts more useful than gum resin.

A popular name for girls in New York is Nevaeh, which is *heaven* spelled backward. At the after-school program in East Harlem where I taught there was a darling little boy named Messiah. I never tired of asking where he was and if he is coming. Oddly, the name Brooklyn has become one of the most popular in the United States over the past few years, just not for babies actually born in Brooklyn.

Growing up I attended the Unitarian Universalist church in Amherst, a suburb of Buffalo, where my minister once made national news for handing out condoms in church at the start of the AIDS crisis. The main difference between Unitarian Universalists and other churchgoers is that the latter claim they have all the answers and want to enlighten you, while UUs claim not to have any of the answers but secretly think they do. They approach life with an open mouth. UUs also differ from others in that they never fast. They believe there is no occasion that cannot be improved with a cheese platter, crudités, chicks on sticks, and carafes of wine. While some people get angry because certain synagogues want hundreds of dollars for a ticket to attend services on holy days, or "pay to pray" as it's known, I like to think that the UUs would initiate a two-drink minimum before charging admission. Otherwise, when it comes to dressing up on Sunday, a few UUs pull on suits and skirts, but many congregants are like me and have their regular jeans and then their church jeans (not to be confused with Jesus jeans, which are holy). The only other way to identify UUs by sight is if a war breaks out – they quickly grab guitars and start singing folk songs in an effort to stop it. A UU friend's Baptist mother summed things up best when she said, "You're like the Episcopalians but worse."

Despite Unitarian Universalism being a small religion (3 in every 1,000 people in the United States), when I moved to the city I had three churches in Manhattan to choose from, in addition to a few more in Brooklyn and Queens. Mostly because it's the closest to where I live, I landed at All Souls on Lexington Avenue and 80th Street. It's the largest and probably the most pragmatic of the three Manhattan UU churches. A number of clergy and laypeople have tried to institute a fellowship handshake at the start of each service, but the attitude of this congregation seems to be that they're already exposed to enough germs on the subway, and if Donald Trump has somehow managed to succeed without shaking the hands of strangers then no one should be obligated to do so. Of equal concern is that we haven't yet come up with a gender-neutral alternative for *fellowship*. (Similarly, our bedtime stories feature a "bogeyperson.")

I've noticed that when we stand to sing hymns a large number of the women keep their purses strapped over their shoulders rather than rest them on the pew or floor, which people would find extremely strange in the church where I grew up. All Souls, or "All Sorts" as we like to call it, also does without the traditional "Joys and Concerns" section of the service where members can stand and share personal news. UUs are inclined to oversharing, and even my small Western New York church had days where Joys and Concerns outstripped the length of the sermon and then some. Instead, this church just lists the number of a therapist in big letters right in the Order of Service. They also tend to say "the historical Jesus" to delineate from the walking-on-water Jesus, unless they spill their coffee, in which case "Jesus" or "Jesus Christ" is still the norm.

As for other UU churches in Manhattan, Fourth Universalist Society on Central Park West is more home-knitted and therefore perfect if you're after a Grover's Corners ambience. They're likely to serve homemade snickerdoodles while we offer Entenmann's out of the box. Community Church on East 35th Street is extra-granola hardcore UU. I mean, we're all on the same page with regard to fighting for social justice, but they're the ones running the Esperanto Society and hosting the Anti-Racist potluck dinners. During one sermon a minister described having a wisdom tooth pulled without any type of anesthesia so she could be "in touch with the pain."

Unitarians often presided over the White House in the old days, a surprising fact considering that they made up such a small percentage of the population. There was John Adams, John Quincy Adams, Millard Fillmore, William Howard Taft, and many consider Thomas Jefferson to have been Unitarian. Freethinkers are out of style these days so I don't think we'll see another UU president in my lifetime. But we did manage to recently get inside the White House on a rug. In 1853, abolitionist and Unitarian minister Theodore Parker said, "The arc of the moral universe is long, but it bends toward justice." In 1963, Dr. Martin Luther King Jr. quoted Parker on the steps of the Lincoln Memorial, and in 2010, President Barack Obama had the words woven into a rug for the Oval Office as King's quote. Another familiar quote on the rug is from Lincoln – "government of the people, by the people, for the people," the well-known phrase from the close of his Gettysburg Address in 1863. However, in 1850 Parker had written something pretty close to what Honest Abe said: "A democracy – that is a government of all the people, by all the people, for all the people." While waiting to come back into fashion, maybe UUs can get jobs as political speechwriters.

It's been more than thirty years since Jesse Jackson referred to New York as "Hymietown" and almost a century since voters rejected Catholic New Yorker Al Smith as president for fear that he'd be a papal puppet. But these days in New York, identity politics has become muted because of the influx of many nationalities, and so has religious politics. There are still a few blocs of Jewish voters in Brooklyn and northern Manhattan, and a large Catholic constituency in Queens and Staten Island, but people mostly vote the issues depending on their conscience and/or economic situation. If there exists a major dividing line in New York it's between those with and without air-conditioning. The melting pot has officially melted.

Am I the only one who finds it ironic that all these bigwigs from Middle Eastern countries who have driven most of the Jews out of their lands come to New York for medical treatment and end up being cared for by no small number of Jewish practitioners? Especially the ones who go to Mt. Sinai Hospital (formerly The Jewish Hospital), with its kosher meals and Shabbos elevators? While they're here someone should tell them about Schleppers movers and Mensch Mill & Lumber.

One local attraction that can be relished no matter your religion, though it may hold more significance if you're a Neo-Druid, is the twice-yearly Manhattanhenge (also known as the Manhattan Solstice). This is when the sun perfectly aligns with the east-west streets that follow the grid adopted in 1811, and observers can watch the globe drop between towering buildings, cast a peachy otherworldly glow, and set upon New Jersey like an alien spaceship. Manhattanhenge usually occurs around May 28 and July 12 or 13 and has been described by astrophysicist Neil deGrasse Tyson as "a unique urban phenomenon in the world, if not the universe." The best views are to be had from the East Side on the major cross streets – 14th, 23rd, 42nd, and 57th. Like so many wonderful city happenings it's free and open to the public and good luck finding a bathroom.

One thing you won't find in New York are any Irish Mormons, not because Mormons are teetotalers but because they believe you're reunited with your family in heaven, and the New York Irish have enough family trouble on earth. Similarly, there isn't much ancestor worship in the city. More than half the population moved here from other places to get away from their parents, and those who were born in the city are waiting for their parents to move to Florida. New Yorkers also tend not to believe in faith healers. If we did, then we'd get them to come over and fix all of our broken phones, computers, and air-conditioners.

Finally, most New York spiritual leaders steer clear of End Times prophecy and preaching the Apocalypse. It's hard to justify needing donations when the world is ending. With regard to the Rapture, New Yorkers would be more concerned about who will take care of the pets that are left behind. Furthermore, religious leaders and politicians in New York have always been careful not to call homosexuality a disease. Otherwise too many people would call in sick for work. Callers would also be quick to point out that the first two letters of the word *Bible* are *Bi*.

Chapter 22

GRAFFITI GOES PRO

It's hard to believe now, but stage performances were forbidden when this city was a Dutch trading post. Those Protestants had no time for frivolity. The English, on the other hand, were heirs to a rich theatrical tradition that began in New York in 1732 when a troupe of actors arrived to perform a series of repertory plays. By the late 1700s, several theaters were in full-time operation, and after the American Revolution the city's first world-class performance space, the Park Theatre, opened downtown. It had room for 2,000 spectators to enjoy circuses, operas, dances, dramas, and musicals, sometimes all on the same program. Times Square, it turns out, was not the first entertainment venue to blur the lines between stage and sex. Theater owners used to allow prostitutes to work the balconies while the police took payoffs or looked the other way.

In the 1840s P. T. Barnum opened his American Museum featuring a wax museum, flea circus, zoo, lectures, variety shows, musical farces, and of course his oddities, which included a bearded girl, little people, the Feejee Mermaid (a mummified monkey's torso with a fish's tail), and the Siamese Twins known as Chang and Eng. Barnum's museum burned to the ground in 1865, but plenty of equally popular, noteworthy, and spellbinding attractions arose to take its place. Going forward, entertainment continued to proliferate with the breakneck expansion of the city itself. How is a century-old Broadway theater different from your local multiplex, you may wonder:

1. There are fewer restrooms. These edifices were built before everyone carried around a personal water supply or 7-Eleven was selling quart-size Slurpees and Starbucks was serving up passion tea lemonade in plastic buckets.

2. There wasn't an NBA in the early twentieth century, and thus people were much shorter and so there's minimal legroom. If you're on the tall side, book an aisle seat. On more than one occasion I've left my orchestra seat and hiked up to the balcony in search of legroom only to find that the six-foot-five-inch Ministry of Silly Walks civil servant, John Cleese, is already there.

3. There aren't any cup holders. Ushers discourage drinking in the theater unless it's one of the $5 bottles of water you bought in the lobby.

My dad's all-time favorite entertainment experience was the 1939 New York World's Fair in Flushing Meadows–Corona Park, Queens. He fondly remembered riding back and forth in what were perhaps the first graffitied subway cars, which had been painted the official blue and orange colors of the exposition. Dad especially liked the futurist automobiles, television sets, and the Billy Rose Aquacade, which offered a preview of Hollywood musical extravaganzas to come. He wasn't nearly as impressed by Smell-O-Vision (movies with odors).

Generally speaking, it isn't until things truly come undone that the work of putting them back together again can get under way. During the 1970s economic doldrums, artists were flourishing in New York's abandoned factories and dilapidated neighborhoods. Music, theater, dance, film, literature, and the visual arts prospered as a result of cheap real estate, a community of avant-garde types, and an atmosphere of artistic freedom. With Off Broadway theaters, galleries, studios, and nightclubs springing up in cut-rate dark corners, the city became a culture engine. It was base camp for abstract expressionism, contemporary art, pop art, plop art (monolithic public sculptures in corporate plazas), minimalists, photo-realistic painters, the vibrant new visual language of graffiti art, underground filmmaking, auteur cinema, Blaxploitation movies, experimental theater, method acting, book publishing, New Journalism, cultural criticism, pioneering TV, observational standup comedy, innovative dance choreography, punk rock, first-generation rappers, figurative sculpture, appropriation art, performance art, and installation art. A couple of high-minded producers decided the addictive nature of television could be harnessed to educate our nation's youth and created *Sesame Street*. A group of irreverent young writers and performers started a variety show that would eventually be called *Saturday Night Live* and not only redefine television comedy, but launch dozens of catchphrases and careers, including that of U.S. senator Al Franken (creator of the "Roman Vomitorium" sketch), all while becoming a New York institution.

Add to that almost everything being done by almost everyone staying at the creatively charged Chelsea Hotel. When these groundbreaking forms of expression were presented to the public they often created "happenings" – the more raw, spontaneous, inventive, and emotional, the better. Much of the art involved nudity. Nude sculpture, nude photos, nude paintings, nude actors on stage, and nude-ins, where you just showed up naked. Perhaps it was the populace's way of saying that there was nothing left to steal, and yet they still had possession of their souls in this city, a modern-day marriage of heaven and hell.

New York may be famous for its theaters, museums, and concert halls, but the performance art everyone talked about in the 1980s were the commercials for the Crazy Eddie tri-state chain of electronics stores. These paeans to poor taste featured an announcer in front of stacks of TVs and stereos screaming, "Crazy Eddie, his prices are INS-A-A-A-ANE." In August, the announcer would wear a Santa suit and have stagehands pelt him with fake snowballs for the Christmas in August sale. This led to direct competition from Mashugana Dave and also Mashugana Ike. *Mashugana* is derived from the Yiddish word for crazy. Because New Yorkers view it as a plus to be crazy, for a long time the stores did well. However, Crazy Eddie eventually went out of business and the founder went to jail for fraud, but the iconic commercials survive on YouTube and in the 1984 movie *Splash*.

Meantime, an indoor Museum of Sex has sprung up to replace the old Times Square outdoor one. And this being New York, its nickname is MoSex. Despite restrictions placed on adult entertainment venues, the authorities have allowed the museum to be within 500 feet of a school, adding a new meaning to "sex education," and within 500 feet of a church, because it's always good to know exactly whom you're praying for. Unlike many of the exhibits at the American Museum of Natural History (and the old Times Square), those at the Museum of Sex are not interactive – a sign warns that in addition to not touching anything, you shouldn't "mount" anything. It's pleasant to have lunch or a snack at the aphrodisiac-themed café, but as you can well imagine, it's hard to get people out of the gift shop, which serves as both entrance and exit.

New York City has almost 100 museums, and it's worth digging into a few off the beaten path to the dinosaurs at the American Museum of Natural History. You need to make an appointment to visit the Lower East Side Troll Museum since it's located inside the apartment of one Jennifer Miller, a performance artist known as Reverend Jen, and the occupant is also the curator. Many of the exhibits were damaged in a 2010 steam pipe explosion, but the good thing about trolls is that abnormalities just enhance their charm. For canal fans there's the Hall of Gowanus, a mini-museum and gallery devoted to the Gowanus Canal. And for Kurds, Kurd lovers, and closet Kurds, a four-story brick house in Prospect Heights, Brooklyn, holds the Kurdish Library and Museum, the only one of its kind in the country.

A student of architecture could spend a year in New York City and still not see every beautiful, breathtaking, brilliant, startling, ugly, neoclassical, Biedermeier, Queen Anne, Richardsonian Romanesque, futuristic, modern, Beaux-Arts, Art Deco, Bauhaus, Usonian, postmodern, sustainable, or What-Were-They-Thinking edifice. The World Trade Center, which opened in 1973, was very much of the last school, though some kindly deemed it "plain." Most said the best thing about it was the panoramic view of New York City from the top, and that from there you didn't have to see the World Trade Center.

At the time of their completion, the original One World Trade Center (the North Tower) and Two World Trade Center (the South Tower), known collectively as the "Twin Towers," were the tallest buildings in the world, and a symbol of American capitalism. On the stunningly perfect morning of September 11, 2001, the quarter mile–high towers collapsed in less than two hours after terrorists drove a hijacked plane into each one. From my window it looked as if Lower Manhattan had gotten its two front teeth knocked out.

A memorial and a museum are now on the former site of the Twin Towers to commemorate the almost 3,000 people killed. From having worked on Wall Street as a trader and a journalist, I knew a dozen people who lost their lives that dreadful day. At least I thought it was a dozen. Upon visiting the memorial, I found the name of another acquaintance I was not aware had died. What's more, the stonemasons inscribed "and her unborn child" after her name, as they did with the names of all those women who were pregnant. This was especially moving; until then I hadn't realized to what extent so many victims had been awaiting new life.

In addition to the memorial and the museum, a new complex of five skyscrapers is under construction to replace the former seven buildings and is, after much debate, also being called the World Trade Center. The new One World Trade Center officially became the tallest building in the United States on November 12, 2013, with a symbolically significant height of 1,776 feet.

In the numbingly sad days and weeks and months that followed 9/11, New Yorkers briefly relinquished any pretenses of exceptionalism, sarcasm, indifference, or toughness and showed that they aren't really different from the rest of the world after all. At heart they're good, decent human beings who were raised to help their neighbors in an emergency, even if they didn't know their neighbors. In addition to the enormous sacrifices made by firefighters and police, there were heroic displays of courage and kindness by average citizens, while assistance arrived from all over the globe in the form of person power, financial aid, volunteerism, moral support, and blood donations.

When we're not busy dealing with real tragedy, Hollywood has always had a particular affinity for decimating New York in order to cream it at the box office. There's an earthquake in *Deluge*; a tsunami and a comet in *Deep Impact*; a rogue planet in *When Worlds Collide*; a meteorite in *Armageddon*; rampant crime in *Escape from New York*; a monster in *King Kong, Godzilla*, and *Cloverfield*; aliens in *War of the Worlds* and *Independence Day*; and global warming in *A.I.* and *The Day After Tomorrow*. On this one I think we'll have to defer to former mayor Koch, who turned to movie reviewing in his later years, and declared that when it comes to New York City the rest of the country has "edifice envy." I'd venture to say that the five unadorned, brown brick, 10-story apartment buildings containing 400 apartments in Flushing, Queens, known as the Bland Houses are a safe bet.

My grandfather was working at a Midtown restaurant in 1930 and always in the market for free entertainment, so standing on the corner of Sixth Avenue and "Toity-Toid Street" during his lunch hour he'd watch the Empire State Building go up. Mohawk Indians known as "skywalkers" worked fearlessly along narrow steel beams fifty stories in the air. These Native American ironworkers also played a large part in the construction of the Chrysler Building, the George Washington Bridge, and the World Trade Center. Grandpa asked one of them why he wasn't afraid to be up so high. The man claimed to be as afraid as the next guy, but explained that he took pride in his work. Then he pointed up to a woman disguised as a man who was filling in so her husband wouldn't lose his job while he was out. Talk about devotion. For more stories about the world's first vertiginous metropolis one can visit the Skyscraper Museum in lower Manhattan's Battery Park City.

I certainly wouldn't suggest visiting New York for its amusement parks, especially since riding elevators, subways, and taxis can be excitement enough, but Coney Island in Brooklyn has recently been given a facelift. Gone are the roving gangs of hoodlums, skittering hordes of vermin, and ramshackle rides operated by half-asleep men who reeked of beer and Limburger cheese. Nathan's Famous, home of the July Fourth Hot Dog Eating Contest, is a survivor along with the historic wooden Cyclone roller coaster that opened in 1926. You can be the judge of whether you want to ride anything that's old enough to have been declared a New York City landmark. Otherwise, there's a new steel roller coaster called the Thunderbolt that boasts a 90-degree drop from 115 feet and speeds up to 55 miles an hour. (Native New Yorkers who spend their lives stuck in gridlocked traffic love feeling what it's like to travel 55 mph.)

However, this big boy is designed for "modern Americans" and therefore skinny people get banged around a bit. Nothing serious, but enough to justify loading up on fried clam strips and funnel cake beforehand. Film buffs might like to know that the original Thunderbolt was featured in the movie *Annie Hall*. And that actor Walter Matthau requested in his will that Nathan's hot dogs be served at his funeral – they were. Now, I can already hear first-time visitors fresh from Six Flags shouting, "You call this place renovated?!" Well, let's just say that after undergoing major upgrades in safety, service, and cleanliness, the area has managed to maintain some of its gritty charm and plus-size rats ("Brooklyn bred, Coney Island fed"). But above all that you can enjoy a wonderful view of where city meets sea from the top of the 150-foot-tall Wonder Wheel.

The Metropolitan Museum of Art is the largest art museum in the world under a single roof, so you should stop in even if it's just to wander through the statue gallery, sit by the Pan fountain, check out the Temple of Dendur, and have lunch at the terrific but reasonably priced (for the Upper East Side) cafeteria. It's worth visiting the Chinese Garden Court because the museum is so large most people never find it and you'll have a measure of solitude there. On the way to the Garden Court, a copy of *Washington Crossing the Delaware* is a must-see picture. Oddly, it was painted by a German-born artist living in Germany. Stranger still, the original was destroyed in Bremen, Germany, during a British air raid in 1942. But what the heck, the Statue of Liberty was made by a French sculptor in Paris. I hope we sent them some subway-token jewelry, pastrami sandwiches, and a case of Dr. Brown's Cel-Ray soda in return.

The interactive show at the Met takes place out front where disabled veterans battle for space to operate pushcarts selling food and drink. They've turned the museum plaza into the Coney Island boardwalk much to the chagrin of the trustees. Some of the city's über entrepreneurs search out disabled vets, who have a special legal right to be there, and pay them to sit in a chair all day in case an inspector comes along while the impresarios do the actual work.

Visiting popular destinations like the Met brings up the subject of living on the other side of the clock in New York. As often as possible in a city of 8 million people, you want to do things when the other 7,999,999 are not doing them, particularly if you work a day job and already have to deal with the madding crowd during the week. Shopping for groceries after work, seeing movies on weekends, and having brunch on Sunday are generally not good ideas unless you enjoy waiting in line. And because of fire codes and limited space, most waiting in line is done alfresco in all kinds of weather, often while being panhandled.

You definitely don't want to shop for toothpaste and shampoo in a drugstore while all the feverish, sneezing, hacking sick people crowd together in the cold and flu aisle, huddle around the staff to sign Sudafed release forms, and pick up their ampicillin. Honestly, I don't think a separate pharmacy for healthy people who just want to buy Band-Aids and vitamins is too much to ask for.

In order not to miss enormously popular attractions such as Madame Tussauds, the Guggenheim, Empire State Building, Statue of Liberty, and Ellis Island (be sure to watch the orientation movie first), get tickets early or else arrive early – early as in you have your nose pressed against the glass when the doors open.

If you're a resident then it's good to keep a "dream list" handy. The minute the city gets all frantic over an inch of snow, bundle up and dash to the museums, trendy restaurants, Tony award–winning musicals, and Shake Shacks that usually have lines around the block. I've had the Frick Collection and Museum of Modern Art (MoMA) all to myself while everyone else was out buying batteries and being fitted for snowshoes. Once while walking through Washington Square Park on a particularly polar-vortexy night I didn't see any of the usual drug dealers, and then suddenly from out of the shadows came a murmur: "Pot, frozen pot."

New Yorkers tend not to go to popular attractions unless forced into action by an out-of-towner. Most residents can't give you directions to the Empire State Building. A couple I know moved to Wilmington and the husband kept complaining that he could no longer go to Broadway shows, art galleries, museums, and the ballet. The wife said he'd never gone to any of those things when they lived in New York. He replied that at least he knew he could. Living in New York you're going to be surrounded by the arts, just like those who reside in Washington, D.C., are immersed in politics, whether they enjoy it or not.

A main reason that aspiring artists continue coming to New York is there are excellent schools here such as Juilliard, Pratt, Parsons, Cooper Union, Tisch, Columbia, American Academy of Dramatic Arts, and the New York Academy of Art. Such a move seems to make sense if you want to dance, paint, act, play music, or make films, but I'm not entirely sure why it's always appealed to writers and poets, especially since one assumes they'd be in search of a quiet place to work and contemplate. There isn't really anything like the famed Iowa Writers' Workshop or Yaddo artists' community, just a few high-powered review outfits such as *The New York Times Book Review* and *The New York Review of Books*, which a writer friend likes to call *The New York Review of Each Other's Books*.

One might think that so many scribblers in one place would have trouble finding an audience or be too focused on the same subjects. Yet they keep arriving and thriving. If everyone here decides to become a writer, who will be left to read? As it is now, a book party is judged successful by the number of friends who show up, and a poetry reading is deemed triumphant if the audience outnumbers the poets who are presenting. Being that most of our resident versifiers call Starbucks their office, the city may have launched what will become famously known as the Caffeine School of Poetry. I'm sure it's just a matter of time before they unionize.

Greenwich Village in particular has been a notable outpost for writers and artists since the nineteenth century. At first it was an elite neighborhood with winding tree-lined streets, fine architecture, and a

European sensibility, but in the 1850s wealthy residents began moving uptown and their former homes were either subdivided or replaced with tenements. Along with an influx of Irish, German, and Italian immigrants, the inexpensive rents attracted artists and intellectuals. New York University, founded in 1831, not only brought prominent faculty to the area but also other institutions such as theaters, art societies, small presses, galleries, and libraries. The freethinking, free-loving atmosphere also attracted radicals, socialists, bohemians, and sex tourists. And no matter the decade, for some reason perhaps known only to Afro-Cubans, the neighborhood has never been short on open-air bongo players.

The Village has been home or hangout to such artists and iconoclasts as Thomas Paine (*Common Sense*), Washington Irving (coined the name Gotham), Walt Whitman ("I am large, I contain multitudes"), Augustus Saint-Gaudens (General Sherman Monument across from the Plaza Hotel), Mark Twain, Edgar Allan Poe, O. Henry, Hart Crane (*The Bridge*), Edna St. Vincent Millay, Eugene O'Neill, Jackson Pollock, Bob Dylan, and Edward Albee. Stephen Crane wrote *The Red Badge of Courage* at 61 Washington Square while working as a reporter. The famous *Nighthawks* painting by Edward Hopper was supposedly modeled on a diner in Greenwich Village, which was the artist's permanent home. Literary luminaries such as Theodore Dreiser, Djuna Barnes, and E. E. Cummings have lived on the gated cul-de-sac off 10th Street called Patchin Place, which is a magnet for psychotherapy offices and known as "Therapy Row." The Village was also where Woody Allen and Joan Rivers performed their first stand-up comedy routines, and Hal Holbrooke rolled out his Mark Twain show.

When I first moved to Greenwich Village in 1984, it was untouched by chain stores, superstores, and souvenir shops. Scattered along its cramped sidewalks containing metal trapdoors every few feet, and mixed in with low-slung apartment houses and numerous gyro/souvlaki joints, was a pell-mell collection of cafés, performance spaces, bars, and cabarets. No matter when you arrive everyone likes to say, "You missed it. You should've been here ten years ago."

Still, I was able to see tenor sax star Sonny Rollins at the Village Vanguard, legendary bluesman Willie Dixon at Kenny's Castaways, and trumpet great Dizzy Gillespie at the Blue Note (who had airbags in his cheeks before we had them in our cars). I sat at tables with beat legends and rabble-rousers such as Allen Ginsberg, Abbie Hoffman, and Jerry Rubin. Comedy Cellar presented the waiting-to-be-discovered Joy Behar, Jon Stewart, Louis C.K., Jerry Seinfeld, Ray Romano, Rita Rudner, and a teenage Chris Rock. Traveling a few blocks east, it was possible to enter the punk rock era at the legendary CBGB and see Patti Smith, Television, the New York Dolls, the Dead Boys, and the Ramones. With torn clothes, sculpted hair, Goth makeup, and safety pins as accessories, punk was being manufactured in New York City the way the blues had gelled in the Deep South a century earlier. Stage diving, crowd surfing, and slam dancing had supplanted the Moon Walk, the Robot, and the Electric Slide. The area was also in an uproar over graffiti artist Jean-Michel Basquiat's provocative social commentary and Keith Haring's politically barbed imagery juxtaposed with childlike characters. (Basquiat would die of a heroin overdose in 1988 at age twenty-seven, and Haring would succumb to AIDS in 1990 at thirty-one.)

It's now being shouted from the fire escapes that Brooklyn is the new Manhattan. Former borough president Marty Markowitz declared his beloved Brooklyn the "Lesbian Capital of NYC and the Northeast" as a way of cementing its LGBTQ cultural currency, and perhaps starting a catfight with Northampton, Massachusetts. Best known in the 1970s for its chop shops and street gangs, these days Brooklyn is the "it" destination for up-and-coming artists and writers the way SoHo was in the 1980s and Greenwich Village before that. Berl's in DUMBO is the only all-poetry bookstore in New York City. No doubt that if Shakespeare were working today, even he would decamp to Cobble Hill right behind Martin Amis. Instead of *The Taming of the Shrew* we'd have *She Thinks Who She Is*, *Henry IV, Part 2* would be *Who Died and Made You Boss?*, Shylock would be Wisenheimer, and *Much Ado About Nothing* would be called *Fuggedaboudit*. But even without the Bard, Brooklyn is pretty confident. There's a sign in the Brooklyn Battery

Chapter 23

TREADMILLS, TRANS FATS, AND TREATMENTS

New York is not usually listed under retirement communities because no one here wants to admit to being over fifty. The city saves a fortune because so few people ask for discounts. You won't see any signs in restaurant windows for early-bird specials. There's a large print edition of *The New York Times* but it circulates on the black market. You don't see a continuous loop of ads for motorized scooters on television in New York because with all the dashing up and down subway stairs, running for cabs and buses, and traipsing several blocks to restaurants, stores, and movies, few people are overweight. In fact, New Yorkers weigh on average six or seven pounds less than suburban Americans.

Same with our kids – there's no December 15 National Cupcake Day for young New Yorkers since city schools cracked down on baked goods in 2009. Meantime, there are few elevators or escalators in ancient New York subway stations, so even if you skip the gym you still get a workout. Good balance is involved since you really don't want to touch handrails or grab bars under any circumstances (remember the disease ads?). Add a baby carriage, luggage, or shopping bags and there's the benefit of a weightlifting component.

On top of our firearms and cigarettes, Manny Bloomberg took away our trans fats, required restaurants to reveal calorie counts, raised the age for buying tobacco from eighteen to twenty-one, made a hard run at our sugary sodas, and tried to put a seven-day waiting period on ordering chocolate chip pancakes. I'm surprised the residents of Toronto didn't attempt to pair up their cursing, vodka-guzzling, overeating, crack-smoking mayor Rob Ford with clean living Manny Bloomberg in a Big Brother program. We're lucky to still have T-shirt cannons at concerts and fireworks on the Fourth of July. You can buy cigarettes on every corner – you just can't smoke them anywhere, including offices, bars, restaurants, subway platforms, parks, and public spaces. Working with Javert-like zeal, Manny Bloomberg managed to ban smoking in bars and nightclubs, afraid that it sent the wrong message to the prostitutes, gamblers, drug dealers, and cokeheads. Smoke-easies have since sprung up around the city where no one complains if you light up and there's a guy on the lookout for approaching health inspectors. New Yorkers are now hoarding chewing gum just in case Manny Bloomberg one day becomes president. The next entrepreneurial breakthrough will come from the person who invents a patch for those having trouble getting off the cronuts.

If it's any consolation, Manny Bloomberg passed a law to have defibrillators installed in public places such as courthouses, municipal office buildings, ferry terminals, stadiums, nursing homes, large health clubs, and some parks and golf courses. But are these machines supposed to make New Yorkers more or less stressed?

Thirty years ago, gyms were dingy, sweaty places filled with equal parts body odor and free weights where boxers trained and ex-cons plotted their next heist. Then actor and former activist Jane Fonda pulled on a striped leotard and leg warmers to start hawking workout videos, Olivia Newton-John's exuberant single "Physical" climbed the charts with the line, "There's nothing left to talk about. Unless it's horizontally," and Calvin Klein's nearly naked underwear models helped fuel a health craze. In a tank top and short-shorts fitness fanatic Richard Simmons brought us snappy phrases like, "A MOMENT ON THE LIPS; A LIFETIME ON THE HIPS," "DON'T DIET, LIVE IT!" and "THIGHS, THIGHS, GO AWAY, GIVE THEM ALL TO DORIS DAY!"

Sleek gyms soon appeared on every block, offering juice bars, piped-in music, and customized workouts, for which New Yorkers gladly shelled out membership fees equivalent to one month's salary. They were just in time since the advent of the personal computer and the Internet would soon strand everyone on the couch shopping, playing video games, Googling themselves, and having webcam conversations on Chatroulette. When I was young and we played outside all day, children were terrified of the dark, but now that they play video games in dark rooms all day long, kids are afraid of the light.

It can't be a coincidence that the nation's first center for head-shrinking found a welcome home here when the New York Psycho-analytic Society and Institute was founded by a group of Dr. Sigmund Freud's disciples in 1911. Getting therapy is not a source of embarrassment for New Yorkers. There are even signs that warn "Depressed Storm Drains." In the nice weather it's not uncommon for lawn chairs to pop up downtown and in the busier parks with average Joes offering free or low-cost advice. There's usually a line. Local bookstores, especially on the Upper West Side (which could qualify as Psychotherastan on a *New Yorker* cover map), devote large sections to therapy and self-help, which is either a sign of robust mental health or of serious instability. I'm always surprised there isn't a bigger market for secondhand therapy. Certainly in a place this populous many folks must be suffering from similar problems. Shouldn't it be possible to walk out of a session and sell what you just found out at a cut rate? I have one friend who's been in therapy for more than forty years to the tune of $500 per week, and she said the summation would be: Do the things that you think will make you happy. That's over a million dollars in free therapy right there and more than covers the cost of this book.

Similarly, there are recovery programs in New York for everything. City dwellers tend to be in a rush, so programs such as AA tend to be six steps instead of twelve. (I've had Jewish friends tell me that because of busy schedules on Passover, the Four Questions have occasionally been shortened to just two or three.) Not surprisingly, New York is the birthplace of "speed shrinking," where panels of therapists, usually armed with their books and business cards, give quick fixes of advice while their harried patients move through a line. New Yorkers don't do anything slow, and they don't single-task. In addition to everyone being a multihyphenate, such as a bus driver–filmmaker–drug dealer, almost everyone is bi – bicoastal, biracial, bipolar, bilingual, biannual (going home twice a year for Thanksgiving and Christmas or Hanukkah), and of course the one you thought of first. Living in a crowded city, people are conscious of limited space and thus thankful we're all biodegradable. The only thing we're not is bipartisan.

The premise of *Ghostbusters II* (1989) was that the collective negativity of New York City's anger was powering a river of slime under the streets, making it possible for an evil sorcerer to take over the city via the body of a baby. It's true that jam-packed Madhattan in particular surely contains a high level of communal fury when you factor in subway rage, bike-lane rage, slow-walker rage, taxi-in-the-rain rage, Razor-scooter rage, stroller rage, parking rage, office rage, random rage, parade-in-my-way rage, subway-grate rage (which afflicts persons in high heels), and lack-of-public-restroom rage.

Speaking of the last: The newspapers regularly run articles on which public restrooms transsexuals use – ladies or gents. I see plenty of transsexuals in New York. They're easy to spot since they don't switch from heels to sneakers for the walk to the subway. However, show me these supposed public restrooms! Restaurants want you to buy something before using the bathroom. Stores claim not to have them. Hotels want proof that you're a guest. Even if you've never read a book, the bathrooms are a good reason to hope that Barnes & Noble doesn't go out of business. New York women live on average seven years longer than New York men. However, they will spend at least six and a half of those years searching for public bathrooms. The Big Apple means Bladder Control. You know something is up when signs everywhere proclaim RESTROOMS FOR CUSTOMERS ONLY and a New York restaurant guide has an entire section called "Bathrooms to Visit."

If you're caught in the Times Square area in need of a restroom I can heartily recommend the Marriott Marquis where you go up several escalators and there's no hassle from security. In Lower Manhattan, head to the National Museum of the American Indian on the south side of Bowling Green, adjacent to the northeast corner of Battery Park. Admission is free, and the downstairs restrooms are terrific. While there, check out the highly detailed Reginald Marsh murals in the rotunda that depict daily life in the city's shipping days. On the Lower East Side, for a scary adventure in bladder relief, enter the crazy quilt of shops known as Essex Street Marketplace. You can get a key from a vendor for a journey up a dimly lit staircase and past some creaking heavy metal doors that look like they once imprisoned the most violent patients in a nineteenth-century mental hospital. Otherwise, if you don't want to spend $12 in a restaurant just to use the restroom, the only other option is to stop in at a doctor's office and ask to leave a urine sample.

New Yorkers aren't ashamed to take medication for their mental health. Instead of swapping holiday recipes, we exchange prescription information. And our favorite party game is: If you were stranded on a desert island with only one medication, which would it be? While gyms are open until eleven p.m., restaurants until midnight, clubs until two or three a.m., most drugstores are twenty-four hour. Basically, Manhattan is a series of apartment and office buildings squeezed between drugstores, coffee shops, and ATMs. I once attempted to get cough syrup in Erie, Pennsylvania, after 9 p.m. Impossible. In Houston I asked for directions to the pharmacy and had to take a twenty-minute taxi ride. In Manhattan, sometimes a Walgreens is opposite a CVS with a Duane Reade around the corner. In the 1980s, Coca-Cola created a mission statement in which they wanted a person never to be more than several feet from a can of Coke. The city of New York feels exactly the same about residents and their medication.

New Yorkers wear their neuroses like a badge of honor. Woody Allen has made an entire career out of his. Even our pets take anxiety and depression medication. A Central Park Zoo polar bear named Gus made headlines around the world in the 1990s when he was swimming figure eights obsessively in his pool for up to twelve hours a day, day after day, month after month. Locals suspected that it was an identity crisis because he didn't know for sure whether he was an East Sider or a West Sider. An animal behavioral therapist was brought in to the tune of $25,000. Gus was pronounced "bored and mildly crazy in the way that a lot of people are in New York City," and an enrichment program was put into effect. Locals felt somehow vindicated that even a bear who seemingly had everything, including an inground swimming pool and daily admiration, was finding it difficult to cope.

It helps somewhat to know that we are suffering collectively. I can guarantee that after every sixteen or so hours of city life you'll have to lie down for at least seven or eight. While most local news magazines run feel-good human interest stories every week, *The New York Times Magazine* has a five-pager about some near-death person with mysterious symptoms that no doctor can diagnose. The editors tease out this medical thriller until we get as close to a resolution as possible because New Yorkers know that there are never any easy fixes. When Manny Bloomberg started the 311 phone line for nonemergency complaints about blocked sidewalks, barking dogs, foul odors, and open fire hydrants, residents immediately began phoning about bad breakups, not getting callback auditions, salary gripes, and flu symptoms.

Whereas people in general have been known to take a certain amount of pleasure when others fail, New Yorkers can be so complex that they're able to have feelings of Schadenfreude about themselves. Of course, with all the prescriptions and therapy, you could easily think this is a city of pessimists. But that's not so, which is why there's a race to cure something in Central Park every five minutes from May until December.

New York City has been vying for the Summer Olympics the past few years. Trust me, people who don't want their own president or any visiting royalty in town definitely don't want the Olympics. For one thing, we're already registered in the year-round New York Olympics. See how you do in the following events:

1. Register a car at the DMV.

2. Get from the Bronx to Wall Street at rush hour.

3. Buy two orchestra seats for whichever musical just won the Tony Award.

4. Find a public restroom in Midtown.

5. Flush a low-flow toilet in fewer than five tries.

6. Commute ninety minutes to and from work.

7. Live with the smell of Korean cooking coming through the airshaft night and day.

8. Eat street meat for breakfast, lunch, and dinner.

Dating is the number one cause of mental illness in New York. If the psychological thriller *Fatal Attraction* has a theme it would be that single life in this city will transform you into an obsessive, kidnapping, knife-wielding, emotional-blackmailing stalker and boiler of bunny rabbits. "City of Orgies" is how Walt Whitman described Manhattan in the 1876 edition of *Leaves of Grass*. With the advent of the Internet, it might more accurately be described as a place where people are lonely together. A million blinking screens and a million broken hearts.

The *Sex and the City* stars had hot and cold running boyfriends. However, gals outnumber guys by 5 percent in the general population, while among twenty-five- to twenty-nine-year-olds it's 10 percent. And why does it feel like there are more gay men than lesbians, further diminishing the female dating pool? To make things worse, due to gender profiling women hardly even get stopped and frisked by male police officers. Single men are always "single" men in New York. Meantime, women in their twenties and thirties are considered "available," but women in their forties and fifties are "alone."

People like to argue that New York women are being too picky and perhaps that's true. When making an online profile it's best to include your neighborhood because people aren't willing to travel that far for the unknown. Although if women really wanted to increase their odds when it comes to husband-hunting, they'd move to Alaska, the state with the highest male-female ratio, or else Afghanistan, where one man can have up to four wives.

There are plenty of activities for singles to connect, including mixers, speed dating, and all types of clubs, classes, and sports, but a lot of people moved here specifically to avoid group activities. For instance, a group of New York teachers, librarians, and booksellers wanted to copy Chicago and other cities by having us all read one book at the same time. The effort quickly collapsed into vicious squabbling. It probably would've been easier to get the entire city to embark upon a juice cleanse together seeing as there are more Jamba Juices than bookstores. Similarly, you won't find many league bowlers in New York, though that may be a consequence of it being a sport with no offense.

Most people who don't meet online find each other in nightclubs, parks, gyms, grocery stores, or during the ginormous December pub crawl known as SantaCon. The subway is also known for being a matchmaker, and in addition to facilitating those who get up the courage to exchange information or make dates, it has spawned a number of websites seeking "missed connections" (e.g., You wore black spandex pants and aviator shades with a blue tint and got on the 6 train at Park and 28th…) à la Charlie Brown and the elusive Little Red-Headed Girl. The only hard and fast rule about dating in New York is never to form relationships with people living in fifth-floor walk-ups since they might ask you to help them move.

When it comes to New York weddings, ushers are careful to ask, "Bride or groom?" rather than, "What side are you on?" since the latter can elicit anything from a West Side–East Side rant to a diatribe on politics, euthanasia, or gay ministers. If it's a same-sex wedding then folks can sit wherever they like as it's a "judgment-free" zone.

Chapter 24

TIME'S WINGED TAXICAB

New York is a place of extremes, where differences are celebrated or at the very least tolerated. You're guaranteed to be welcomed but not necessarily loved. People of every age, class, ethnicity, profession, sexual persuasion, political leaning, philosophical view, religious belief, fashion choice, and personality disorder are on display. They crowd the streets, sidewalks, public spaces, office buildings, parking garages, subways, buses, train stations, elevators, museums, theaters, shops, bars, and restaurants. On constant parade is the whole spectrum of human nature, and it turns out there's a whole lot of human nature to go around. There's no detour past it or private plane over it and no gate on this community. In contrast to *Survivor*, on our islands we don't take a weekly vote regarding who gets to stay and who has to go. A number of extraterrestrials have even walked among us unmolested and unprobed, according to Preston Dennett's "true history," *UFOs Over New York*.

Contradictions are therefore not resolved but rather contained within the sprawling tapestry of daily life. If there's not always a communal sense of Whitmanesque belonging, then there's the certainty that we're all in it together. This was exemplified by how the ravages of 9/11 made no distinction between executives and interns or accountants and janitors. Victims were mostly residents of New York, New Jersey, Connecticut, and Pennsylvania, but they had origins from around the country and the globe. Emergency workers who lost their lives were not just from Manhattan but from all five boroughs, in addition to Long

Island and Upstate New York. We were revealed to be more connected than we'd thought.

Talking heads insist that incidents such as the Trayvon Martin trial are going to lead to a "conversation on race." New York has been having that tête-à-tête daily since 1626 when slaves first arrived in the colony. Stand in a crowded subway car, that great equalizer, and look around. You will see every ethnicity, along with professionals dressed to the nines, groups of yawping students, riders rocking baby carriages, hipsters, Hasids, civil servants, and blue-collar workers along with folk showing off their tattoos, body piercings, and hair sculptures. If that subway car gets stuck overnight in a snowstorm as happened in 2011, you are suddenly one big freezing-cold family, sharing supplies and figuring out a lavatory plan together. No shouting or panicking, no robberies or cannibalism occurred, just understanding and cooperation. Sure, there are laws, courts, cops, and firefighters. But 8 million locals are moving about alongside another 2 million nonresidents who commute each weekday, plus the tourists and day-trippers. The system must sustain itself based upon a million unspoken mutual agreements. Hundreds of unsung tender mercies occur every day, including daring animal rescues, assisting confused visitors, and offering spare rooms to homeless people. Many altruistic efforts succeed, leading to saved lives and fresh starts. In my friend Suzy's case, the homeless man offered an alcove in which to sleep and stay warm stole her bike.

New York has as many optimists as pessimists. The optimists keep us all moving forward, smiling as we attempt to navigate around construction sites and movie shoots, all working together toward a better and brighter future. And the pessimists, with their withering sarcasm and "why bother" attitude, all share a little secret – once you give up hope you start to feel better.

Compared to the doomsday machine the city resembled when I arrived in the 1980s, it's now in a respectable phase that boasts safer streets, better schools, cleaner air, and more parks as well as playgrounds, bike lanes, ferries, tour buses, subway stops, skyscrapers, sports stadiums, smokeless bars, coffee bars, cigar bars, sports bars, gyms, galleries, clean cabs, chic hotels, chain stores, box stores, flagship department stores, sidewalk cafés, refurbished piers, indoor malls, Silicon Alley, street fairs, farmers' markets, high-rise condos, the High Line, billiard parlors, public spaces, day spas, museums, concerts, theaters, Shake Shacks, cupcake shops, food trucks, gluten-free pizza, wine tastings, night clubs, penthouse soirées, spin classes, hot yoga, power yoga, kids' yoga, yogurt bars, smoothie shops, beekeepers, microbrewers, pickle-makers, cronut bakers, baristas, fashionistas, hipsters, e-smokers, metrosexuals, brunch lovers, superstars, poseurs, wannabes, locavores, party planners, Russian tycoons, clipboard people, Vespas, Razor scooters, Bugaboo strollers, Segways, personal trainers, life coaches, spiritual advisors, animal whisperers, bloggers, and preservationists. And of course pharmacies. When Duane Reade is out of something the salespeople ask, "Did you try our store across the street?" Meantime, the pursuit of adult entertainment and designer drugs is arranged mostly online and out of sight.

Above all, blessed are the double-decker tour buses, for they are truly a private enterprise serving the public good. In the 1980s tourists were free range and on the loose, standing at the top of every subway stairwell looking bewildered, stuck in every revolving door, clogging up subway turnstiles, monopolizing token booths, trying to give bus drivers dollar bills, asking visibly disturbed homeless people for directions, and getting lost, mugged, and swindled. My friend Neil refers to such hominid logjams as CPUs – Central Pennsylvania Units. Counter-tourism measures became a local government priority. Nowadays these holidaymakers are safely packed onto coaches, waving, smiling, and snapping photos, and being watched over by enthusiastic young people who are paid to care for them. I am always happy to be stuck behind or give way to a tour bus. I'm even happier to show my houseguests where to board the bus and without fail suggest the three-day pass, which includes Manhattan at night, Brooklyn, and the Bronx.

Remember the Bowery Bums? For better or worse, the Bowery has become one of the city's chicest streets with boutique hotels, tony apartment buildings like Avalon Bowery Place, and upmarket clothing shops. High-end men's clothing designer John Varvatos took over the location of the famed CBGB club. Journalists are always chronicling the passing of the last veteran to have served in World War I or World War II, but what about the last shopper to have exited the revolving doors of famed department stores such as Gimbels or Wanamaker's?

And whoddathunkit but some of New York's old graffiti, which authorities worked so hard to thwart and remove, now resides in museums or on the streets in preservation programs. You can *pay* to go on walking tours that feature graffiti and street art in Manhattan, Brooklyn, Queens, and the Bronx.

New York is no longer home to the world's largest population, tallest building, longest bridge, most crowded subway, or busiest seaport. But for much of the last century New York City has been the financial, cultural, media, retailing, and fashion capital of not just the country but the world. It's a progressive town. Whereas other places are just now getting around to Casual Friday and Take Your Daughter to Work Day, New York has already moved on to Cross-Dress Friday and Take a Lesbian to Lunch Day. Meantime, New York doctors don't want to tell expecting parents the sex of their baby so much as let it decide for itself when it's a teenager.

With steam billowing up from the manholes, sewers, and subway grates the city appears to be one giant percolator. Feel that New York high. It's real, a result of all the antidepressants and mochaccinos that have leached into the water table. It's just a matter of time before coffee shops open counters inside of drugstores.

We're all merely placeholders, observing while being observed. We've learned that you stand "on line" and not "in line," a person plays "piano" and not "the piano," Houston Street is pronounced "Howston" Street. Public housing is known as "The Projects." The Naked Cowboy is not entirely naked and most likely not a cowboy. We understand that when Upper West Siders say the "Met" they mean the Metropolitan Opera, when Upper East Siders say it they mean the Metropolitan Museum of Art, and when Croatians say it they mean Middle European Time. (Under no circumstances does it mean the "Metro," which is always the "subway" or the "train.") We've stood at the intersection of Waverly and Waverly and we know that the main branch of the New York Public Library doesn't allow you to take out books. We try to avoid the Long

Island Rail Road on Memorial Day weekend at all costs. We wonder why New York windows don't have screens. And where have all the gas stations gone?

The celebrated tic-tac-toe-playing chicken left the Chinatown Fair arcade in 1998 under pressure from animal rights sympathizers, despite being a consistent moneymaker. The chicken, always a female, won many more games than she lost. Rest assured, the last one (Lillie) did not end up as a local menu item but went to a farm in Massachusetts. Meantime, the Algonquin Hotel cat, who wandered in one night in the 1930s, proves that cats indeed have nine lives. Male replacements are named Hamlet while females are called Matilda. The hotel celebrates his/her birthday with a party on July 10th every year. The current Algonquin cat, Matilda, has her own e-mail address if you're interested.

The one constant throughout New York City's history has been its ability to change, adapt, and reinvent itself. Restless energy is a defining characteristic. When the circus comes to town, there are plenty of residents and tourists to greet it in the middle of the night, and there's also a bevy of animal rights activists protesting the event. The American Stock Exchange is being turned into a boutique hotel with specialty shops as I write this. It took New Yorkers less than a month to incorporate the city's bicycle sharing program (aka Mike's Bikes) into cycle-themed weddings. The Citi Bikes are borrowed, blue, and new, so that's three out of four right there.

As old buildings are demolished and rent-controlled apartments disappear, a new real estate controversy has arisen in large part thanks to the Internet. Websites such as Airbnb, which match visitors with tenants willing to turn their apartments into short-term rentals, are getting kudos from New Yorkers who need extra income as well as from travelers on a budget, while landlords, neighbors, and the city's hotel industry cry foul. This has created a whole new generation of apartment dwellers who are sneaking around, trying not to be found out. No wonder this town has always been such a magnet for talented actors.

New York has a long history of renaming its roads, theaters, neighborhoods, and airports. Crown Street became Liberty Street after the American Revolution. Laurens Street became South Fifth Avenue and then West Broadway. Around 1847 a potter's field was named Reservoir Square, and in 1884 it was renamed Bryant Park in honor of *New York Evening Post* editor and abolitionist William Cullen Bryant, and then nicknamed Needle Park when it served as an open-air drug market in the 1970s (though it was far from the only city park with that designation). Today, Bryant Park is a convivial urban paradise and home to wholesome square dances, carousel rides, holiday fairs, a free ice-skating rink, outdoor movies shown on a supersize screen, and an open-air library with Wi-Fi access. Best of all, they have fabulous free restrooms with mosaic tiles, mirrors framed in cherry wood, fresh-cut flowers, and electronic seat covers. Longacre Square became Times Square in 1904. Being that a world record was recently broken in Herald Square it will surely be rechristened Twerking Square in the near future.

The area known as Little Germany is now the East Village. The Gashouse District became Stuyvesant Town. The San Juan Hill neighborhood was demolished to make way for Lincoln Center. Hell's Hundred Acres is now SoHo. The Number 7 train line to Queens has been dubbed the Orient Express due to a recent surge of Asian immigrants. The Globe Theater on West 46th Street became the Lunt-Fontanne. The Virginia Theater was renamed the August Wilson. There's a Facebook page called "Tennessee Williams Deserves to Have a Broadway Theater Named after him." And why not? As his most famous character Blanche DuBois famously said, "I'm only passing through." We're all just passing through. The stately brownstone that was Edith Wharton's childhood home on West 23rd Street is now a Starbucks. Mafia don John Gotti's headquarters in Ozone Park, Queens, has become a pet-grooming salon.

The largest of the new buildings on the 9/11 site was originally called the Freedom Tower. But in 2009 it was rechristened One World Trade Center for one of the two towers destroyed in the terrorist attack. So that address lives on for another day.

The infamous Flatiron District disco/drug den the Limelight was originally built as the Church of the Holy Communion in 1844, counting John Jacob Astor, Jay Gould, and Cornelius Vanderbilt among its parishioners. A century later a commune called the Lindisfarne Association took up residence, only to pack up for Colorado after a few years. The Odyssey Institute, a drug-counseling organization, bought the property from the Episcopal Church and sold it to nightclub operator Peter Gatien in 1983, one assumes without the drug counselors. After Gatien's Limelight nightclub closed in 2001, an investor who'd taken a stake in the club when Gatien fell behind on his mortgage payments gained control of the property, and it's since been transformed into a mini-mall (with restrooms on the third floor!). One can buy a Lacoste shirt on the same spot Andy Warhol, Elton John, and Madonna did the Hustle (and heaven knows what else), and where robber barons once prayed that it would be easier for a rich man to get into heaven than for a camel to go through the eye of a needle.

While some buildings have undergone several name changes over the decades, there are others such as the longstanding Broadyke at the corner of Broadway and Dyckman Streets that probably should. Perhaps the nearby Broadyke Meat Market feels like it's time for a transformation as well.

New York is famous for comebacks. If we're going to have a motto on city license plates it should be: The Bigger the Setback, the Greater the Comeback. The 1970s hit movie *Saturday Night Fever* returned as a 1990s Broadway musical. Johnny Carson's *Tonight Show*, which fled midtown Manhattan in May of 1972, returned to the place of its birth in February of 2014 with new host Jimmy Fallon, after almost forty-two years in Los Angeles.

Bedbugs were common in New York until the 1950s, when fumigation, better hygiene, and improved sanitation made them a rarity in all but the most squalid settings. People used to coat their bedposts and headboards with petroleum jelly or soapy water to stave off the advancing army. I grew up hearing my father warn me, "Don't let the bedbugs bite," despite my never having encountered such a creature. Well, they're back, in housing projects, hospitals, posh townhouses, and swank department stores. And so lots of bedbug-sniffing beagles are hanging out their shingles. Grandpa loved saying, "A recession is bad for the shoe salesman but good for the shoe repairman."

In March 1925, construction workers digging a building foundation near Broadway and Dyckman Streets, just blocks from where my dad was born, discovered the jawbone of an American mastodon that included fourteen teeth. Paleontologists believe that mastodons, saber-toothed cats, and woolly mammoths were quite prevalent in the area during the last ice age, about 18,000 years ago, but abruptly disappeared a few thousand years later. Maybe they're preparing for a comeback too.

Richard Nixon came to New York to rebuild his image following his resignation after the Watergate scandal. After a life of political upheaval, Madame Chiang Kai-shek, one-time first lady of the Republic of China, landed on the Upper East Side, where she died in 2003 at the age of 106. New York was where Judy Garland would have numerous "comeback concerts" in the 1950s and '60s. ("And to hear the press tell it, a comeback every time I went to the powder room.") Famous silver-screen icon Greta Garbo retired to Manhattan, which might be considered an odd choice considering she said, "I want to be alone" or "I want to be left alone" or both. But you can be alone here, and also never feel lonely. In 1949, E. B. White famously wrote that New York City bestows "the gift of privacy, the jewel of loneliness." Were apartment walls, ceilings, and windows thicker back then?

There are 20,000 people buried under Washington Square Park. We come and work and play, and they build over us. We are beings in our time. We live surrounded by history, knowing that generations have walked these same streets before us and generations will follow, God willing as the Irish like to say, or goddess willing, as the New Agers like to say.

The cosmopolis remains forever a mystery and a marvel, inspirational and infuriating, arousing both loathing and longing. Whether you're a resident, visitor, or commuter, your New York is different from everyone else's. If you've come here to find yourself, they say to see who everybody else is and you're what's left over. Henry Hudson was one of the few people to not find what he was looking for and leave New York dissatisfied back in 1609. I guess that everywhere is always going to be someone's nowhere. Meantime, the Pilgrims were aiming for the mouth of the Hudson River but went off course. We could all be wearing big hats, rectangular white collars, and buckles the size of Bibles.

What have I gleaned from this amazing adventure? It was told to me by an airline counter attendant at JFK Airport during the black-out of 2003. She said, "I've learned that the only thing I can control is my own behavior." And surely philosopher William James was thinking about New York when he wrote, "Wisdom is learning what to overlook."

Old Lady Life is what's happening right now on our native clay. The sirens, the jackhammers, the garbage trucks at four a.m., the ferret devotees, the breathtaking sight of the Brooklyn Bridge, the jaw-dropping view from the Brooklyn Bridge of imperious steel and stone fortresses with gleaming glass and delicate silvery spires where heaven meets earth. As purple dusk rises from the sidewalks the stars overhead are splashed by the vaporous glow of streetlamps and a radiant Times Square. Wayfarers from around the world saunter out in search of a dream, an answer, a fix, or someone to hold.

Is the past what we take with us or what we leave behind? Either way, nothing will ever be like it used to be. And it's all over before you know it. The city rushes to cover our tracks. Too bad and thank goodness.

ABOUT THE AUTHOR

Laura Pedersen is a former *New York Times* columnist, the author of fifteen books including the award-winning humorous memoir *Buffalo Gal*, and a playwright. She has appeared on *Oprah* and David Letterman, performed stand-up at the Improv, and writes for several well-known comedians. Her award-winning play *The Brightness of Heaven* ran at New York's Cherry Lane Theatre in 2014. More info is available at **www.LauraPedersenBooks.com** and Facebook/Laura Pedersen Writer.

ACKNOWLEDGMENTS

Much appreciation to Fulcrum publisher and Renaissance Person Sam Scinta for his continued support and encouragement, resident marketing mavens Melanie Roth and Jess Townsend, editor extraordinaire Alison Auch, editor in chief Rebecca McEwen, and cover designer Alex Asfour. A big shout-out to *The Elements of the Story* author Frank Flaherty for sharing his New York knowledge. Many thanks to the talented Jim Schembari for his keen editorial eye. Also to my early readers and reviewers, Aimee Chu, Judith Ehrlich, Barry Goldsmith, Steve Newman, Neil Osborne, Sophia Seidner, and Willie Pietersen. Ongoing appreciation to publicity prodigies Wiley Saichek and Meryl Zegarek.

CRITICAL ACCLAIM
FOR LAURA PEDERSEN

Beginner's Luck

"Laura Pedersen delivers…if this book hasn't been made into a screenplay already, it should be soon. Throughout, you can't help but think how hilarious some of the scenes would play on the big screen."

—The Hartford Courant

"Funny, sweet-natured, and well-crafted…Pedersen has created a wonderful assemblage of…whimsical characters and charm."

—Kirkus Reviews

"This novel is funny and just quirky enough to become a word-of-mouth favorite…Pedersen has a knack for capturing tart teenage observations in witty asides, and Hallie's naiveté, combined with her gambling and numbers savvy, make her a winning protagonist."

—Publishers Weekly

Best Bet
"The book's laugh-out-loud funny, and readers will find themselves rereading lines just for the sheer joy of it."

—Kirkus Reviews

The Big Shuffle

"Although it's a laugh-out-loud read, it's an appealing, sensitive, superbly written book. One you won't want to put down. I loved it."

—The Lakeland Times

"Be prepared to fall in love with a story as wise as it is witty."

—The Compulsive Reader

"A breezy coming-of-age novel with an appealing cast of characters."

—Booklist

Buffalo Gal

"This book is compulsively readable, and owes its deadpan delivery to the fact that she has performed standup comedy on national television (*The Oprah Winfrey Show, Late Night with David Letterman, Today, Primetime,* etc.)."

—ForeWord Magazine

"...[Pedersen's] wicked, sarcastic, dry, self-deprecating sense of humor won me over and I absolutely loved it start to finish."

— Printed Page

Fool's Mate

"*Fool's Mate* bounces along and then proceeds at a taut, riveting pace as the cast of characters in this cleverly-crafted novel love, learn, and grow in a way that gives new meaning to folly and wisdom! Delightful!"

—Crystal Book Reviews

Going Away Party

"Pedersen shows off her verbal buoyancy. Their quips are witty and so are Pedersen's amusing characterizations of the eccentric MacGuires. Sentence by sentence, Pedersen's debut can certainly entertain."

—Publishers Weekly

Heart's Desire

"Funny, tender, and poignant, *Heart's Desire* should appeal to a wide range of readers."

—Booklist

"Prepare to fall in love again because Laura Pedersen is giving you your 'Heart's Desire' by bringing back Hallie Palmer and her entire endearing crew. In a story as wise as it is witty, Pedersen captures the joy of love found, the ache of love lost, and how friends can get you through it all—win or lose."

—Sarah Bird, author of
The Yokota Officers Club

"This book will make you laugh and cry and like a good friend, you'll be happy to have made its acquaintance."

—Lorna Landvik, author of
*Angry Housewives
Eating Bon Bons*

Last Call

"Pedersen writes vividly of characters so interesting, so funny and warm that they defy staying on the page."

—The Hartford Courant

"This book is a rare, humorous exploration of death that affirms life is a gift and tomorrow is never guaranteed. Pedersen writes an exquisitely emotional story. A must-have book to start the new year."

—*Romantic Times*

Planes, Trains, and Auto-Rickshaws

"Pedersen captures the zeitgeist in exploring the personal side of India."

—*Buffalo News*

"Deft mixture of facts and humor whets the appetite for a visit."

—*JWR*

Play Money

"A savvy insider's vastly entertaining line on aspects of the money game."

—*Kirkus Reviews*
(starred review)

The Sweetest Hours

"To call *The Sweetest Hours* a book of short stories would be like calling the *Mona Lisa* a painting."

—*Front Street Reviews*

"Pedersen weaves tales that blend humor, sorrow, and sometimes surprise endings in the games of life and love."

—*Book Loons*